RAKU

RAKU

by Christopher Tyler and Richard Hirsch

55490

WATSON-GUPTILL PUBLICATIONS/NEW YORK

PITMAN PUBLISHING/LONDON

Copyright © 1975 by Watson-Guptill Publications

First Published 1975 in the United States and Canada by Watson-Guptill Publications,
a division of Billboard Publications, Inc.,
1515 Broadway, New York, N.Y. 10036

Library of Congress Cataloging in Publication Data
Tyler, Christopher, 1944—
    Raku, techniques for contemporary potters.
    Bibliography: p.
    Includes index.
    1. Raku pottery. I. Hirsch, Richard, 1944—
joint author. II. Title.
TT920.T93 1975   738.1   75-11934
ISBN 0-8230-4503-X

Published in Great Britain by Sir Isaac Pitman & Sons Ltd.
39 Parker Street, London WC2B 5PB
ISBN 0-273-00912-5

Manufactured in U.S.A.

First Printing, 1975
Second Printing, 1977

To Arline and Rosemary
for their understanding and patience

Acknowledgments

The craftsmen who helped us in the making of this book are warm human beings, unselfish, dedicated, and cooperative. In a sense, this is just as significant as the information they provided. The sincerity with which they approach their own work was reflected in the honest attention they gave to ours. We found them to be our "well spring," not just for the data, but because of their refreshing attitudes and personalities. While we corresponded with them individually, a composite image was formed in our minds. It was of a group of people from all over the world belonging to a unique family that strives for innovation within the realm of its rich tradition. To all of them we express our gratitude.

Within this context special appreciation is extended to Paul Soldner, Howard Yana-Shapiro, Wayne Higby, Daniel Rhodes, Neil MacEwan, Norman Kerr, Joan Campbell, and Hobart Cowles. In addition we want to particularly thank True Kelly for her photographs of the Winter and Summer Tea Bowl demonstrations in Chapter 3. Finally, we would like to express our deep gratitude to Robert and Marguerite Antell, without whose generosity this book could not have been written.

Contributing Craftsmen

Marguerite Antell
Nancy Baldwin
Sister Celeste Mary Bourke
Winn Burke
Joan Campbell
Wendell Castle
John Chalke
Hobart Cowles
Ken Ferguson
John Frisenda
Henry Gernhardt
Jean Griffith

Art Haney
Wayne Higby
Nancy Jurs
Jun Kaneko
Susan and Steven Kemenyffy
Marilyn Levine
Ann Mortimer
Josh Nadal
Albert Paley
Daniel Rhodes
Laureen Shaw
Marc Sijan

Kit-Yin Tieng Snyder
Paul Soldner
Bill Stewart
Dave Tell
Carol Townsend
Peter Vandengerge
Ken Vavrek
Frans Wildenhain
George and Betty Woodman
Mutsuo Yanagihara
Howard Yana-Shapiro
Adele Zimmerman

Contents

Preface

How easy it is to be solemn! To write a few pages tracing every detail of how we did our how-to-do-it book! After the rigors of writing on a subject, how tempting it is to bore the reader with sincerety and believe that he will be fascinated by our opinions on the high points of, as well as the faults and omissions in, the manuscript. If the following comments seem written in this manner, it's probably because the personal nature of introductory comments invites the indulgence.

We would like to be able to record a blinding flash which marked the conception of this book, in the manner that Gibbon was able to record the exact beginning of *his* book:

It was at Rome, on the 15th of October, 1764, as I sat musing amidst the ruins of the Capitol, while the barefooted friars were singing vespers in the Temple of Jupiter, that the idea of writing the decline and fall of the city first started to my mind.

However, our efforts can be traced to no such moment. Moreover, neither of us has the slightest recollection of how the idea to write a book on raku began. All we can say is that out of friendship, proximity, and mutual interests, the book grew.

As we worked on the book, we came to share almost all aspects of it, until is was impossible to say who was responsible for this part or that. Gradually, however, it became clear that final decisions on the various elements of the book allocated themselves, more or less, to our personal strengths. Rick had the final word on the technical information and visual matter; Chris handled the text and took some of the photographs. The majority of the content, however, was arrived at through long hours of joint discussion. Every decision was made through consultation. Memories of writing the book center on these times—resting with a pile of books on a log by a pond or sitting in a boat drifting down the St. Mary's River, talking or reading back a draft of a previous discussion.

The growth of the total concept of the book was a joint effort, too, though this involved several other people. In particular, a meeting with Daniel Rhodes at the home of Marg and Bob Antell provided us with a strong foundation for attacking the book. It was not only Daniel Rhodes' advice, though this was invaluable, but also his presence and personal philosophy that made us aware of the responsibilities of authorship and the need for quality and accuracy.

A colleague put us in touch with the publisher. Two conversations with Don Holden of Watson-Guptill helped us recognize the audience for the book.

But of all the influences on us, Paul Soldner's has been probably the strongest. In response to our questions, he made a cassette recording of his recent opinions on raku. His understanding of the medium is, as one would expect, most subtle, and his understanding of the quietness and strength of raku awakened sparks of recognition in our minds.

Probably the most vivid experience in our work on this book was a few days spent in the company of Howard Shapiro at the Naples Mill School of Crafts in Naples, New York. Rumors of a strange character had reached us—"Hey, man, have you heard of this dude who pulls out raku pots with his *bare* hands?"—but we were not prepared for the unstinting generosity, friendliness, compassion, and honesty of the real man. The freshness of the days spent with Howard Shapiro, and also with True Kelly as she photographed him, remains with us and, we believe, altered the book.

But writing the book was not all happy meetings and idyllic boat rides. The most difficult thing of all, and it occupied us from the beginning to the end, was to fix the level of the book. Ideally, we wanted to reach both the novice and the potter teaching graduate students. These people required different kinds of information, and we wanted to reconcile them. What we did more or less was to address an intelligent newcomer to raku (though not necessarily a newcomer to clay), setting down everything we had found out about raku. The university student in pottery hopefully would be stimulated by the clarity of restatement, and by our attempt at a more comprehensive treatment of the subject than has been attempted before. We gave information necessary for the beginner to make raku pots. However, we were a good way toward solving this dichotomy in realizing that to stress direct contact with the materials and honesty to the process of raku will always be essential: even the most elementary details may be important to novice and sophisticate alike. Deciding what to leave out was a difficult part of the writing. We did not want the book to be over-technical, nor did we want it to be a book of pictures. We wanted it to be *read* and worked with.

The correspondence with many potters took a lot of time, but it provided an invaluable source of opinion about raku. We chose to quote from these letters frequently and feel we succeeded in being fair to all sectors of opinion. Our debt to those potters who took the time to respond to our questions in writing is immense. We felt that through their words we were able to provide a balance to our own views about raku. This was complemented by the visual material in the book, the whole providing a survey of contemporary work in raku.

In this way, by striking a balance between our views and others' and by blending philosophy and technical details, words, and images, we hope to have made a useful book.

The book falls short, though, of being the definitive work on raku. Our lack of experience of Japan and Japanese raku is greatly felt, though the help of the Royal Ontario Museum in allowing us to handle and drink out of their tea bowls, went a little way toward offsetting this deficiency. An ideal, definitive work on raku would undoubtedly incorporate more information and photographs dealing with Japanese raku. Similarly, our coverage of European trends could have been stronger, and there are a couple of American potters we could not contact, whose contribution would have rounded out the material.

An introduction should be brief, because as a rule few people read it. Let the exception to this rule be only on the reader's side; suffice it to say that we enjoyed making the book; we hope it will be read and will give as much pleasure in its use as it gave to us in its creation.

Chris Tyler
Sault Ste. Marie, Ontario, Canada

Rick Hirsch
Boston, Mass.

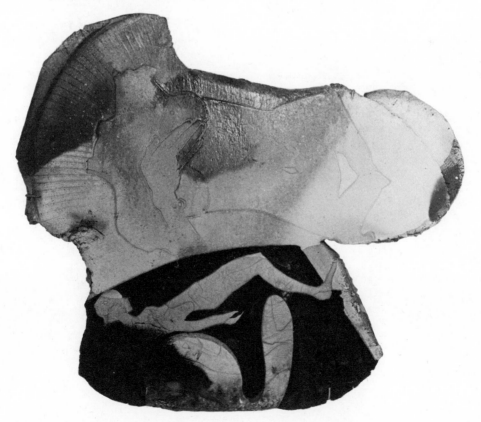

Plate *by Paul Soldner. Slab construction, partially glazed, engobes and metal oxide, smoked.*

Tea Bowl, *raku ware. 4 15/16″ (12.5 cm) high. Japan, Edo period, 18th c. Dark gray with thick black orange peel glaze. A typical winter tea bowl, showing a strong, simple form. Attributed possibly to Nonko.*

1

The History of Raku

Raku is one of the genuine examples in art history of a development that can be called "original." It is also one of the few art forms which has not suffered in its revival—rather, it has been strengthened. When raku began in the latter half of the 16th century in Japan, it represented a fresh direction of human endeavor, both technically and aesthetically, and the intrinsic possibility of the medium led to its revival with fresh aesthetic impetus in the 1960s in the United States. Naturally, like most original developments in history, raku has its traceable causes, but the coincidence of impersonal causes and of human creativity is sufficiently complete that we may say that at a certain time a characteristic form of pottery was created where nothing like it had existed before.

The original Japanese pieces of raku were tea bowls, and the raku potters worked exclusively to produce vessels for the tea ceremony. It is impossible to deal with the origins of raku out of the context of the Japanese tea ceremony and of its involvement with Zen Buddhism, as the simple experience of sipping tea from a raku tea bowl is invested with significance from these sources.

Zen Buddhism

Buddhism, of which Zen Buddhism is an offshoot, was first introduced into Japan in 552 A.D. Buddhism at this time was a sophisticated religion with nearly 1,000 years of development behind it. Its existence in Japan established in the fabric of society the practices of contemplation, retirement, and enlightenment through the power of the mind. Generally speaking, this form of Buddhism offered salvation through a rejection of this world, and by a complete faith in something beyond oneself.

Zen Buddhism was brought to Japan and established there principally by two celebrated sages: Eisai

(1141–1215 A.D.) and Dōgen (1200–1253 A.D.). In China, Zen Buddhism (or as it is called there, Ch'an Buddhism) had been the principle form of Buddhism from as early as the Sung period (960–1279 A.D.), and Zen at that time was heavily involved in the general dissemination of Chinese culture. Zen Buddhism is by its nature impossible to express verbally,[1] and finds its most eloquent expression in cryptic anecdotes about holy men, and in the arts, of which the tea ceremony is an important branch.

Zen does not have a body of doctrine but is an approach to salvation—a way only. Self-discovery through contemplation is the main "method"; Zen aims to end the classic human dualism in the ordinary man, and to find an ultimate union of body and soul, of the individual and the rest of creation. This aim of ultimate union takes several forms, of which it may be useful to mention some here.

One of the surprising things about Zen, yet an important reason for its spread, is its ability to reconcile worldly tasks with a deeply spiritual belief. For example, Zen monks were active in diplomacy and politics and after the ruling Shogun Ashikaga Yoshimitsu (1358–1408 A.D.) appointed a Zen devoté to lead a foreign delegation, every subsequent delegation was similarly led; local leaders in Japan also employed holy men for official political purposes within the country. For the person following Zen's way, life itself became an art which was understood as "the discipline of creative labor," making use of man's only possession—time.[2] It is not surprising that Zen manifested itself partly in a ceremony—an ordinary social event, taking place in time as well as space.

Besides the world of politics, the world of nature is embraced by the Zen follower. The Japanese love of nature found a natural outlet in Zen, and developed into a love of asymmetry and roughness which contrasts particularly

Tea Bowl, *Chi-chou ware. 2″ (5 cm) high, 5 3/4″ (14.6 cm) in diameter. China, Sung Dynasty, 960–1279* A.D. *Buff stoneware with brown glaze with tortoise shell mottles of yellow and blue-gray on exterior; interior with two phoenixes and two six-petaled flowers reserved in brown on cream-flecked ground. This elegantly shaped tea bowl indicates the refinement of form sought by the Chinese.*

Tea Bowl, *Chien ware. 2 11/16″ (6.8 cm) high, 4 3/8″)11 cm) in diameter. China, Sung Dynasty, 960–1279* A.D. *Black stoneware with thick brownish black glaze with hare's fur markings. A good example of a Chien ware tea bowl of the type exported to Japan. The hare's fur (tenmoku) glaze with the thick roll near the foot has a thick, succulent quality.*

Tea Bowl, *raku ware. 2 3/16" (5.5 cm) high, 5 1/4" (13.3 cm) in diameter. Japan, 19th c. Gray earthenware with thick black orange peel glaze. Raku stamp.*

Tea Bowl, *raku ware. 2 7/8" (7.3 cm) high, 4 1/2" (11.3 cm) in diameter. Japan, 19th c. Overall mottled glaze, basically of light green but blushed with orange particularly on upper portions; pinholes in glaze. This bowl embodies all the typical characteristics of a raku tea bowl—a rolling rim, an organic, asymmetrical form, a pockmarked glaze which is not melted uniformly, a foot that elevates the bowl properly, and a spiral on the interior to collect the last drops of tea.*

Tea Bowl, raku ware. 3" (7.6 cm) high, 5" (12.7 cm) in diameter. Japan, Edo period, late 18th, early 19th c. Buff earthenware with thick, dark brown, orange peel glaze; the body shows buff where the glaze is thin. Of the three Raku stamps on the exterior, two are abbreviated. A very opulent, voluptuous tea bowl which invites you to touch and hold it. The rim has a pleasantly soft outline.

A detail clearly showing the abbreviated and full seals.

with a Western, neoclassical love of symmetry and proportion. The Japanese traditionally do not favor a matched pair—a typical "pair" in Japan might be a tortoise and a crane,[3] where the balance is achieved by the height of one and the lowness of the other. Japanese raku, and the environment of the tea ceremony, often borrows from the roughness of rocks, allows for the flow or stillness of water, or remembers the undulations of mountain ranges.

The Zen belief in the union of all things shows itself most clearly in one of its most important aesthetic concepts, and Japanese raku is clearly enriched by it. The word *yugen* is used to refer to an ultimate quality in art, and is in some ways close to our "symbolism" except ultimately in its reference. The Western symbol, where it has not been influenced by Eastern art, mostly refers to *something*, probably an abstract concept, such as Virtue, or Christ as Savior, and assumes to some extent a correspondence between the form and the abstract "meaning." *Yugen*, on the other hand, is found despite the material form, and the form is kept as simple as possible in order not to distract our mind from the silent, unspecific, final reference. The simplicity of Japanese art is often stressed, but not perhaps in this light—Japanese art is often simple in the sense of being utterly direct; i.e., the work makes an essential statement, and needs not convolutions of form to express a direct vision of the truth. De Bary quotes from Mumyo Hisho as an example of the circumstances and emotion of *yugen*:[4]

It is just as when we look at the sky of an autumn dusk. It has no sound or colour, and yet, though we do not understand why, we somehow find ourselves moved to tears.

Much of the simplicity of the tea ceremony has its roots in the Zen notion of *yugen*.

Zen Buddhism needs symbolic, not just spoken, communication, sees daily life as being of supreme importance, and must achieve a simplicity and directness of expression. It would seem inevitable, then, that Zen Buddhism in Japan should produce, as perhaps its most representative flower, something such as the tea ceremony.

Tea and the Tea Ceremony

The tea plant was brought to Japan by Eisai, the same man who brought Zen Buddhism. The association between Zen and tea drinking was formalized in the latter part of the 15th century by Murata Juko (1423–1502 A.D.), known as "the father of the tea ceremony." Tea drinking had previously been advocated for medicinal purposes, and was also associated with the trappings of the Imperial Court in Kyoto. Juko responded to the burgeoning influence of Zen at this time, and applied the concept of *wabi* to the tea ceremony. The Japanese use the word *wabi*, variously translated as "simple," "retiring," or "austere," to denote an important quality in Teaism. This reaction to the aristocratic flavor of the ceremony up to this point, took the form of an appreciation for natural things in response to the influence of Zen Buddhisms.

Coinciding with the rise of *wabi* in general taste, and probably connected with it, was the rise to influence of a new class. The *samurai*, roughly equivalent in status to the medieval English knights, came to comprise about 6% of the population of Japan. They first became politically prominent in the 12th century, and by the Kamakura period (1185–1333 A.D.) were an established force in provincial Japan. They lived a simple, frugal life, and in their dual activities of farming and warfare were close to the land and to death. Their austere virtues stressed self-discipline and fine character and, it has been suggested, caused them to be particularly attracted to Zen. The austerity caused by their military duties and the simplicity of agrarian life certainly affected their aesthetic sensitivity, and this class was influential later in popularizing the tea ceremony.

The tea ceremony in its final form was conceived by Sen-no Rikyu (1521–1591 A.D.). It involves a tranquility conducive to contemplation, restricted conversation, and a chosen setting with chosen utensils. The specially made tea house is a simple structure, small, often thatched, and stands in a quiet part of a garden. The events in the ceremony are simple, and the movements and posture of the participants are formal but relaxed. A poem and a flower arrangement hang on a wall for the pleasure of the guests; the utensils are sometimes costly but are always chosen for their proper beauty. Raku tea bowls are among the most important of the accouterments and are highly prized. Connoisseurs tasting the water to be used in the tea ceremony prefer to try it out of a raku bowl. The tea ceremony is still performed today but is, in the words of one commentator, "embalmed," and it appears generally agreed that the original spirit and seriousness of the ceremony have to some extent died out.

An important constituent in the ceremony is naturally the tea itself. By Rikyu's time it was in powder form and was whisked into froth in the tea bowl, thus determining the shape of the bowl to some extent. The taste of the tea also determined the total experience of the ceremony, and has been well described as follows:[5]

Tea is bitter . . . The tea always tastes the same, and yet each bowl is slightly different; the nuances of substance are its essence . . . it always plays upon the nuances of sense, a dialogue between perception and raw or but slightly formed material.

At what was probably its height of excellence in the 17th century, the tea ceremony was a sophisticated, yet simple, form of worship, of self-development, and of art and life appreciation. Each part of the ceremony and setting has the possibility for spiritual significance. This is particularly true of the tea bowl which was used during the most intimate transaction in the ceremony. Dōgen, the second Zen master, said:[6]

Tea Bowl, Zeze ware. 4 3/8″ (11 cm) high, 4″ (10 cm) in diameter. Japan, Edo period, 17th c. Overall thick dark brown orange peel glaze. Tong marks which show competence in handling the hot bowl are felt to be a beautifying factor. The mark on this bowl is very well done, and is the only decoration on what is otherwise a very severe piece.

Tea Bowl, raku ware. 4 15/16″ (12.5 cm) high. Japan, Edo period, 18th c. Dark gray with thick black orange peel glaze. Design in black glaze on buff of two simple outline houses. This is an unusually heavily decorated tea bowl. The bowl would be rotated with this side towards a guest before he drank, as a courtesy and an invitation to enter, as it were, the tea house.

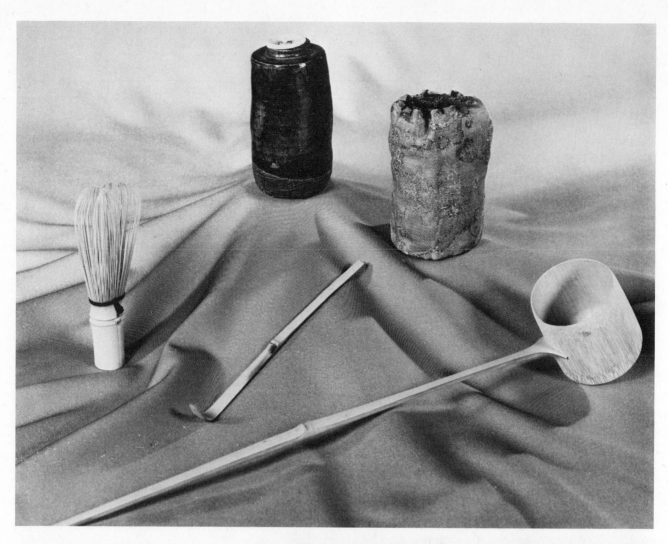

Tea Caddy *(above), Oribe ware, and bag, bamboo scoop, ladle, and whisk. Japan, late 16th c. An arrangement of typical implements used in the tea ceremony.*

Howard Yana-Shapiro demonstrating the tea ceremony.

If you want to obtain a certain thing, you must first be a certain man. Once you become a certain man, obtaining that certain thing won't be a concern of yours any more.

Partaking in the exacting tea ceremony makes one into a certain man, and the appreciative use of the tea bowl contributes to the user's existence.

The Vessel

The Raku family made only tea bowls specifically for the tea ceremony. But before the first Raku was commissioned to make a tea bowl, the vessel itself had undergone considerable evolution.

A Japanese potter named Toshiro went to China in 1223 A.D. in the company of Dōgen. The potter particularly admired Sung celadon ware and Chien-yao tea bowls, identified by the glaze known in Japan as *tenmoku*. From this point, there is an important connection between Zen, the tea ceremony, and Japanese pottery. When Toshiro returned home to Japan, he began to make imitations of celadon and *tenmoku* ware, and it is here that the origin of the tea bowl in Japan is found.

The Muromachi period in Japan (1333–1572 A.D.) was one of heavy Chinese influence. The Chien-yao ware which Toshiro had liked, as well as native imitations of it, was very popular in Japan. Coming from Chien-ning in Fukien province, Chien-yao bowls were stoneware, characterized by their hard or flowing, perfect forms, and the oil spot or hare's fur glazes. Tea bowls were also imported into Japan from Korea during this period.

During the latter half of the Muromachi period, the influence of the *wabi* school of tea, begun by Murata Juko, gradually changed the taste in tea bowls. The growing favor of *wabi* led to a greater appreciation of the rougher Korean tea bowls of the Yi dynasty, and the demand for the more refined Chien-yao (*tenmoku*) ware grew less. Korean Yi dynasty ware had a particular influence on Japanese pottery such as Karatsu, Shino, Oribe, Iga, and Raku. One of the most revered tea bowls in Japan is the Kizaemon Ido tea bowl from Yi dynasty Korea, illustrated in Yanagi's *The Unknown Craftsman* (see Bibliography).

As a result of the many factors contributing to the popularity and importance of the tea ceremony, additional pressure was put on Japanese potters to start making utensils for the tea ceremony such as tea caddies, tea bowls, food dishes, water jars, and incense boxes.

Political events, however, produced a situation which finally stimulated the emergence of raku. The civil wars, which had been occupying Japan for centuries, were virtually brought to an end by three men of military success: Oda Nobunaga (1534–1582 A.D.), Hideyoshi (1536–1598 A.D.), and Tokugawa Ieyasu (1542–1616 A.D.). Each built on the achievements of the previous ruler, and each depended ultimately on his military might and political abilities for his power. The second of these, Hideyoshi, was responsible for encouraging and sponsoring the tea ceremony. It has been suggested that Hideyoshi did so in order that, by creating an artificial value to *objets d'art* connected with the tea ceremony, he would be able to use intrinsically valueless rewards to keep control of his compatriots. Whether this is true or not, Hideyoshi remains at best a questionable figure aesthetically. He was interested in the arts in a troubled time, built sumptuous castles, and was bold enough to order a "tea ceremony" in Kyoto in 1587 that was attended by thousands over a tenday period.

Hideyoshi patronized the tea master Sen-no-Rikyu, who favored the Yi dynasty Korean ware but was finally responsible for an important development in Japanese ceramic history. He commissioned a Kyoto potter named Chojiro to make a tea bowl for the tea ceremony. This Chojiro was the first man to make raku, although the family name Raku, signifying "pleasure," "enjoyment," or "ease," was given by Hideyoshi to Chojiro's successor, Jokei. Chojiro was the son of a Korean[7] father and a Japanese mother, both potters. Accounts of his previous experience vary; some say that he only made roof tiles—itself a trade needing sculptural skill if they were of the ornamental variety, and involving practice with low-fired earthenware. Some sources say that Chojiro was heir to a short but respectable tradition of pottery in his family. If he was of Korean descent, as seems likely, it is tempting to suggest that his father's influence was responsible for the simple, rough qualities in his pots that Rikyu liked. Chojiro's bowls are appreciated for the tactile experience they offer, particularly the way they sit in the hand.

Traditional Raku Glazes

Chojiro used black and transparent glazes for his tea bowls. The black glaze was made from special stones found in the river Kamo. Kamogawa stone is still used as it is apparently a satisfactory material containing a natural mixture of iron and silicic acid. The black comes out as a result of a sudden freezing of the iron in the stone. Its extraction is rapid, but just how it is done is still a secret. The temperature of the water used to cool the glazed, fired pot also remains a secret transmitted from master to disciple. The supply of kamogawa stone, however, shows signs of being depleted today.

Chojiro produced what is known as red raku by the use of a transparent glaze over a yellow ochre slip. The ochre contains metallic elements in its grain which turn red when oxidized.[8] Originally, in the bisque firing, carbon deposits would sometimes be made on the pots where they were stacked close to one another. These random carbon marks show through the glaze and are often prized. Later, a white glaze was added to the traditional repertoire.

The Raku Family Influences

The first three Rakus—Chojiro, Jokei, and Nonko (Donyu) are generally considered the best potters of the line. (Possibly the finest tea bowl in North America, the *Golden Beetle* in the Seattle Art Museum in Seattle, Washington, is by Nonko.)

It is fascinating to speculate about the relationship between Rikyu and Chojiro—how far did Rikyu prescribe for Chojiro what should be made? Rikyu was a sensitive, intelligent man, not only a tea master but also a poet. To what extent was he liable to interfere? Many sources suggest that Chojiro's pots are, at least to some extent, a product of Rikyu's sensibility. On the other hand, Howard Yana-Shapiro, a craftsman who has worked in Japan, met Raku-san, and handled Chojiro bowls, feels that Chojiro undoubtedly was a conscious craftsman. So the question remains: Was Chojiro an unsophisticated craftsman who did what he was told by Rikyu? Or was Rikyu wise enough to see the peasant and unsophisticated qualities of *wabi* in Chojiro's work, and not to interfere? This is an important question when one has to consider the original spirit of raku, for Chojiro's pots tempt one to decide how much self-consciousness went into their making.

Raku Tea Bowls

To summarize traditional raku tea bowls is seemingly easy, because they have so much in common. Not only were they all designed for the same function but also the process is restricted: all were made without the wheel; they all have a foot and an irregular rim; there is no handle; most have a depression inside to collect the last drops of tea. Traditionally, the glazes are limited to black, "red," and sometimes white, and they are all fired in the same way, although the black is much higher fired. Finally, because they are all meant to be held in the hand, the size is relatively similar.

Despite all these similarities, however, when faced with the task of generalizing about tea bowls, one can only throw up one's hands. They are so dissimilar. To handle a tea bowl is important, for the tactile exploration of the surfaces reveals the character of a raku tea bowl in a way that visual examination cannot do. It is through a tactile examination that one can come closest to the essence of raku pots.

Each tea bowl makes its own rules for handling and for drinking position. You find naturally where the lip is. Your hands fit the holding positions.

Memory is insufficient for these tea bowls—they are so subtly irregular that you have to reacquaint yourself with the pot each time you handle it, or drink out of it. You cannot draw it, because a drawing would only be of one side, one face, or one mood. The undulations are too subtle to reproduce. Often, the outside and the inside of the tea bowl relate closely to one another—you realize that they are literally the two surfaces of the same piece of material, and it is right that they appear to be so.

When struck with the fingernail, a raku tea bowl absorbs sound, unlike stoneware or porcelain which has the distinctive ring of being high-fired. This coarse sound, characteristic of low-fired ware, is an indication of the pot's spirit, and just as the pure ring from porcelain is part of its rigidity and, as it were, of its remoteness, so the dull thud of raku seems to indicate its ability to interact at the human level.[9] Raku tea bowls are not refined in the terms of an aesthetic delineated by a single standard of perfection, but in the terms of the aesthetic of imperfection—of the acceptance of all existence—raku does achieve considerable refinement. Often, a raku tea bowl will appear ugly when placed, motionless on a shelf in a museum. But upon close examination, you may find that its beauty depends on a combination of movement, form, time, and handling. A raku tea bowl is a relationship between accident and planning, indicating a complete acceptance of the limits to human decision.

As we find it impossible to generalize further, we would like to give some personal comments on just one bowl. It is an example of all tea bowls, in the sense that all tea bowls have entirely personal characteristics, and description of one may serve to underline the individuality of all. We picked this one because we liked it most of those we have handled and drunk out of, and we have learned enough not to judge a bowl from a photograph, or even from its appearance in a glass case.

The tea bowl illustrated here is a tall, black bowl attributed possibly to Nonko, the third Raku. It has a painted decoration of a house, perhaps a tea house, on one side. On the side opposite the house, the glaze is very waxy. On the outside and the inside there is a wavy line of thick, grayish glaze. The first thing one notices about the bowl is its large size, and its apparent clumsiness. Once held and turned around in the hands, this bowl, when containing liquid, stimulates imaginative comparisons with a lake and mountain tops. The interior and exterior decoration relate to one another, the relationship changing according to how the bowl is rotated or tilted. The liquid held in the bowl also moves and flow out from the interior decoration to the exterior, and to the drinker.

Compared to an English tea cup, a Japanese tea bowl reveals a totally different aesthetic. Less obviously delicate than its Western counterpart, the Japanese tea bowl reflects a more relaxed, or, at least, a less brittle, social situation.

Other Raku Forms and Potters

Other potters besides those of the Raku family were also making low-fired earthenware in the raku manner from the 16th century onwards. Some of the most beautiful and famous tea bowls were not made by the Raku family, and while the founders of the technique were preoccupied solely with tea bowls, other potters branched out

Warren A. Gilbertson, probably the first American potter to exhibit raku and one of the earliest Western authors on the subject, in his studio in Japan, 1938–39.

into other forms and other functions. Even at this stage in its history, raku lent itself to divergence of function and renewed interpretation of form.

Of the many raku-type wares, some were named after the kilns or kiln sites they came from, while others were the recognizably individual work of a known artist. Of these, Honami Kōetsu (1558–1637 A.D.) and Ogāta Kenzan (1663–1743 A.D.) are among the most famous, and both these potters had close connections with the Raku family.

Kōetsu's pots rival those of the Raku family and are famous inside and outside Japan. He was a generally cultivated man, a scholar as well as an artist, and a most influential figure even in his own time. Kōetsu learned most about pottery from Nonko, the third Raku. They are believed to have been friends, Nonko supplying Kōetsu with materials and sometimes even firing his pots for him. Kōetsu's bowls, however, are most unlike Nonko's and vary greatly in their range of expression. They are held by the majority of Japanese experts to express Zen, and were made for Kōetsu's own use rather than for sale. Among his most famous bowls are Fuji-san and Sepo (White Cap). Kōetsu's grandson, Koho, also made raku tea bowls of high quality, mostly red, though one black one has survived. When Kōetsu died, Koho received his grandfather's book of notes on raku which had been acquired from Nonko.

Ogāta Kenzan was a ceramist working in many areas besides raku, and founded a ceramic family of his own. Besides being related by blood to Kōetsu (Kōetsu was his great-uncle), Kenzan became his direct heir in ceramics. When Kenzan was 20 years old, Koho, Kōetsu's grandson, was 82. Koho passed on Kōetsu's book of notes to Kenzan. In this way, the experience of the third Raku, Nonko, was inherited by Kenzan. Apparently, some matters in the notes were difficult, so Kenzan went to Ichinyu, the fourth Raku, and received help from him. Kenzan I, then, possessed a rich inheritance in the knowledge of raku from two sources—by the possession of notes derived from Nonko, and by direct contact with Ichinyu. Kenzan's education in Raku was completed by a close friendship with Ninsei, an older potter who developed overglaze enameled stoneware which is remarkable for its brilliant colors.

While having access to the Raku family's techniques, Kenzan I developed a raku which typically consists of bright pigments on a creamy body. The painterly quality of Kenzan raku contrasts with the more sculptural treatment of the tea bowl by the Raku family and by Kōetsu. The last traditional Japanese potter of the line, known principally for his work in raku, was Ogāta Kenzan VI (1853–1923).[10]

Later Developments in Japan

Travelers to Japan, who knew of the old Japan, frequently comment on how the country is changing, almost beyond recognition. The impact of history has been hard on Japan, wrenching its society through changes of unusual magnitude, and swinging its people between aloof independence and an eager readiness to adopt the customs of others. Naturally, these events have been reflected in raku ware since it was first made.

A damaging criticism of the traditional Japanese raku has been made by Yanagi, who maintained that even in Chojiro's work there were elements of a kind of self-conscious striving for primitivism that compared unfavorably with the genuine simplicity of the Korean rice bowls. As time went on, and perhaps as a result of Japan's isolationist policies from the middle of the 17th century to the 19th, the tea ceremony and the raku ware which was made for it undoubtedly became prescribed and captivated by "rules" for enjoyment and meditation.

Contemporary results of this growing self-consciousness have taken divergent forms. The present Raku-san is not an obscure tile maker, but a self-conscious artist who was trained as a sculptor in an art school. Howard Yana-Shapiro says that Raku-san makes sculpture from which to drink tea.

In Kyoto there is a raku factory which is apparently anathema to Raku-san himself. In the factory, the tea bowls are wheel thrown and consciously altered.[11] According to Shapiro, who worked there for a short time, there are several potters employed in the factory. Each potter is responsible for the entire forming of each bowl he throws, but has nothing to do with the firing. The two firings are supervised by specialists, who have no other job besides their particular firing. The carbon marks on red raku, once a genuine accident of the bisque firing, are now created by a specialist who arranges charcoal sticks around the ware in his electric bisque kiln.

Both these developments seem to be consonant with recent changes in Japan and elsewhere; being the recipient of many generations of traditions brings with it certain pressures to continue and retain these traditions consciously, while a steady demand for one's product may create efficiencies of double-edged value. For various reasons, most of them uncontrollable, Rikyu's original intention seems to have been lost in the self-conscious pursuit of the simple, the plain, the unagitated, and the humble.

In the estimation of the Japanese, raku has not been very popular, according to Yanagihara. "It is," he says, "extremely rare for Japanese potters to use the term *rakuyaki* (raku ware) as a steady or constant expression. The reason for this is because the ceramic tradition in Japan is rooted in the beauty of utility, not style, not in specific glaze." He goes on to say that, because of this, raku has not been employed for very much besides the tea ceremony, although the Japanese have found limited use for raku as tableware, or for vessels for *ikebana* (flower arranging).[12]

Despite this lack of popularity, tea bowls can be very expensive, suggesting that they enjoy the status of exclu-

Raku Vase by Paul Soldner.

Raku Bottle by Paul Soldner. 7 3/4" x 6 1/2" (19.7 x 16.5 cm). Wheel thrown and altered, unglazed, gray and white. These two pots exemplify Soldner's belief that monumental pottery does not necessarily have to be large stoneware.

sivity. John Chalke, a craftsman who has been to Japan a number of times, and has been interested in tea bowls for some time, states that modern tea bowls can cost $3,000 or even $5,000 at 1974 exchange rates, for mediocre pots by well-known people. He feels that pots between $100 and $1,000 are usually more realistically priced.[13]

Much contemporary raku in Japan is not of the traditional kind, however. According to Yanagihara, the interest in raku of "technical ceramic artists," as individual potters are termed there, has been the result of their exposure to American developments in the medium. It is curious that Americans have helped the Japanese rediscover the medium they first invented; many modern Japanese potters are trying to restore the spirit of their tradition with a mighty effort and it is reported that contemporary raku in Japan is in the process of a strong and reassuring renaissance.

Western Developments

It is one of the most astonishing facts in the history of raku that the name Kenzan VII is shared by an Englishman, whose work has quite literally altered the direction of both Japanese and Western pottery.

Bernard Leach. Kenzan VII, or Bernard Leach, as he is better known, went to Japan as a painter and etcher, and after becoming acquainted with pottery through raku (he tells this delightful story in *A Potter's Book*, see Bib-

liography), he apprenticed with Ogāta Kenzan VI and was chosen by his master to succeed him and continue the name, together with Kenkichi Tomimoto. The tradition of continuing an artistic family through a father to an adopted son is important in Japan, and the adoption of a Westerner in this way is a virtually unprecedented compliment.

Leach studied both at the Slade School of Art, and at the London School of Art, and went to Japan in 1909 after reading the works of Lafcadio Hearn. He studied closely with Kenzan until 1915, learning the traditional raku as it had been transmitted in that family. From 1915 to 1920, Leach set up his own kiln, working principally in raku and keeping in close touch with Kenkichi Tomimoto, who also became an eminent Japanese potter. In 1920, Leach returned to England and founded the Leach pottery at St. Ives in Cornwall. He continued to make raku, though his interest in slipware and stoneware, also begun in Japan, gradually supplanted it as his primary medium of expression. From 1920 to 1925, however, Leach held afternoons open to all who visited his workshop in England, and introduced the Western public to raku for the first time. Just as Leach himself was introduced to raku, he allowed his visitors to "paint the biscuit"; the wares were fired on the spot, and sold. This was done with, he says, "no good results,"[14] meaning perhaps that either the pots produced in this way were not good, or that raku did not really grow in popularity. Since 1925,

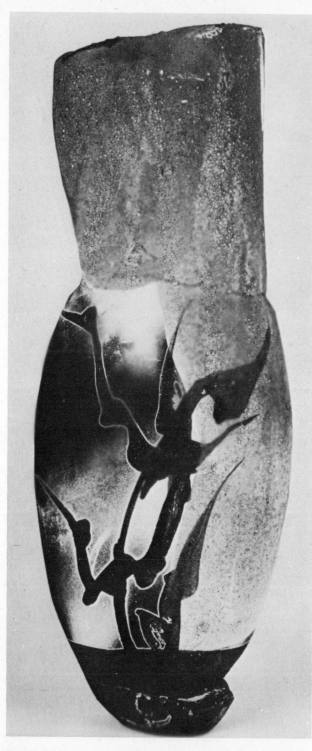

Raku Vase *by Paul Soldner. Engobes, metal oxide, and brush decoration. This pot is a combination of asymmetrical balance, poured engobes, and calligraphic brush work.*

Leach does not seem to have worked much in raku. He feels that the best examples of his pre-1920 work in Raku are in the Tokyo Folk Craft Museum and the Kurashiki Folk Craft Museum. In the West his influence as a potter is vast in the production of stoneware and in the establishment of the craft as an art form, but has been less important as far as raku is concerned.

Besides having a full and busy life as a potter (born in 1887 and still hale and productive, Leach held a show in Japan in 1973), Leach has made a major contribution to ceramics as an author. *A Potter's Book*, first published in 1940, has become prescribed reading for most potters. In this book, Leach gave the traditional methods and recipes for raku which he had learned from Ogāta Kenzan VI, together with a drawing of a raku kiln. By 1940, then, an indirect but reliable link between the Western public and the methods of the original Raku family was established.

Warren Gilbertson. A further link with the American public was provided by Warren A. Gilbertson. Gilbertson has been mentioned before in connection with the history of raku, but his influence is difficult to estimate because his early death in a car accident in 1954 removed him from the craft scene before the interest in raku revived. However, Gilbertson belongs in this history, not only because he was the first American to work in raku, but because, had he lived, he might have become a major influence in American ceramics.

Briefly, his career was as follows: Born in 1910 in Wisconsin, he later studied at the Art Institute of Chicago, at the Carnegie Institute in Pittsburgh, and taught at Hull House. He worked initially as a sculptor (probably in clay) and exhibited two or three pieces almost biannually at the Art Institute of Chicago during the 1930s. He held a one-man show at the San Francisco World's Fair in 1939.

In 1938 he went to Japan to study ceramics and worked for two years with Kanjiro Kawai, mainly in stoneware. However, he became interested in raku and worked with a maker of raku, presumably in Kyoto. We do not know who this was, though it may have been Raku-san himself.

Part of the results of this stay in Japan is an unpublished, hand-lettered book with photographs pasted in as with an old-fashioned family snapshot album. The book is called *Photographs and Notes on Traditional Japanese Handcraft Productions* (see Bibliography). It contains information on stoneware and raku, including a raku glaze formula.

The other immediate result of Gilbertson's trip to Japan was a one-man pottery show at the Art Institute of Chicago. No photographs remain of any of his exhibits at the Art Institute, but the *News Releases* of this show report that it contained tea caddies, covered boxes, vases, tea pots, cups and saucers, dinner plates, etc. Of the 350 pots exhibited, 340 were sold. This fact was commented on in an enthusiastic review which recognized the pio-

Raku Pot *by Paul Soldner. 16″ (40.6 cm) in diameter. 1965. Engobes and metal oxide decoration, copper glaze. A magnificent example of Soldner's feeling for the affinity of form and decoration.*

Paul Soldner firing at his home in Aspen, Colorado.

neering nature of Gilbertson's work, and we can conclude that the show itself was a small but significant landmark in American ceramics. There is, however, no information available in the Art Institute about whether raku was included in the show or not. Daniel Rhodes, though, in his book on kilns (see Bibliography) states that raku was included in the show. This and other evidence lead us to suppose that this show in Chicago, from November 15 to December 29, 1941, probably included the first examples of North American raku, and may have been the first official show of raku outside Japan. The show also included a Japanese wheel and tools.

Gilbertson's contribution to raku is more verifiable, however, in the form of an article by him published in the *Bulletin of the American Ceramic Society* entitled "Making of Raku Ware and its Value in the Teaching of Beginner's Pottery in America" (see Bibliography). This contains a clear description of the raku process and has excellent diagrams of permanent and portable raku kilns. It contains most of the elementary knowledge one would need to know in order to make raku pots. Unfortunately, perhaps, for the development of raku, the process is treated as being mainly useful for instructing beginners—an arguable view which has since developed into a stigma. This article, however, provides the first specifically American source of knowledge about raku, though its influence is difficult to measure.

Gilbertson went on to do an M.F.A. at Alfred University, and worked with the Talavera potters in Mexico. He set up a studio in Santa Fe and succeeded in duplicating the Sung oil spot glaze. In December 1952, he worked with Leach, Hamada, and Yanagi at Craftsmanship Today lectures in Santa Fe. It is impossible to measure the extent of the loss to the craft world when Gilbertson was killed not long afterwards. Certainly, his career as an exhibitor at the Art Institute and other places, and as a teacher and author must at least have left a residual influence. His obituary laments "one of the most highly skilled technicians in the country."[15] Certainly his death removed the potter who was the most knowledgeable about raku in the United States at that time.

While Gilbertson's contribution must remain a matter of guesswork, the mainstream connections go back to Leach, and to a younger man than either: Paul Soldner.

Paul Soldner. Soldner's own account of the origin of his involvement in the raku process is curious, having parallels in its fortuitousness with Rikyu's contact with Chojiro, and with Leach's introduction to pottery through this ware. Certainly, in each case, the circumstances allowed a new direction in pottery to take place.

Soldner's knowledge of raku before he began working in the process was limited to Leach's account in *A Potter's Book*, and Leach's description of the lighthearted, casual way in which he was introduced to raku seems at first to have been transferred in Soldner's mind to the medium itself. The circumstances out of which grew

Raku Vase by Paul Soldner. 9″ (22.9 cm) high. White engobe with metal oxide decoration.

Raku Piece by Paul Soldner.

Raku Vase by Jean Griffith.
18 1/2″ (46.9 cm) high. 1963.
Jean Griffith was one of the first Americans
to experiment in raku post-firing.

Soldner's involvement with raku were as follows:[16] In 1960 he was preparing to give a demonstration of some aspects of ceramics at Scripps College, California. He wanted to do something different from his usual demonstration, and when pressed to be more specific by the students he was talking with, he suggested, on the spur of the moment, that they try raku.

Two factors important to this history emerge from this: First, that there is a definite, acknowledged, connection between the work of Leach and that of Soldner through *A Potter's Book*; and second, that the American originally thought of raku, in his own words, as "a kind of a game"—an intelligent, but essentially lightweight, form of ceramics.

For the demonstration, Soldner and his students prepared stoneware, bisque-fired cups, and Leach's lead glaze from *A Potter's Book*, using cobalt, iron, and copper as stains. They built a 9″ (22.9 cm) gas kiln fairly close to a fishpond and under some pepper trees in a courtyard of the college.

The first firings were successful technically, and everybody enjoyed the dash to the fishpond to quench the newly fired pots. Soldner himself, however, missed in the pots the subtleties written of by Leach. The colors were garish and the clay "pasty." He then had what he calls a "hunch." Knowing that reduction might mute the colors, he plunged a pot into some pepper leaves in a gutter nearby, thereby creating a reduction atmosphere. The results were pleasant and much more subtle. This seems to have been the beginning of post-firing reduction in raku.

It is interesting that Soldner had not seen a genuine piece of Japanese raku at that time, and continued with his own interpretation of the process described by Leach for four years before seeing some tea bowls in the Freer Collection in Washington, D.C. From 1960 to 1964, then, Soldner was investigating the possibilities of raku, and doing workshops, without knowing the extent of his departure from the traditional methods and without knowing the differences of his pots from the traditional kind. A potter of great ability, responding to the barest description of a process, and allowed to investigate the possibilities he perceived, Soldner created a fresh direction. It is tempting to ascribe an almost magical influence to raku. Soldner himself describes this new beginning as "serendipitous" and happening "in a raku way." Certainly, this feeling informs his own pots to a large extent.

Soldner's basic process has not altered much until recently, and in essence remains the standard procedure for most modern raku potters. He himself, during that first three-day workshop, made up a clay body which he says he has not substantially changed.

One other element needs to be mentioned to complete the coincidental, or inevitable, transformation of raku in 1960. Soldner had for some time been doing large stoneware pots with undoubted success. He did feel, however, that the value judgments of the time tended to restrict "serious" pottery to stoneware and porcelain, and that this undervalued the possibilities of earthenware. We can conjecture that the potter and his time were especially receptive to the possibilities of such a medium: overglaze lusters, low-fired earthenware, bright commercial low-fired glazes, and decals, all began at about the same time, and Soldner's involvement with raku seems to have been part of a general new direction in low-fired ware.

Nothing, however, can hide the important fact about Soldner's contribution to ceramics and to raku: by using deliberate post-firing reduction, Soldner discovered a way for the potter to continue to create his pot after firing. This follows naturally from the particularly intimate contact with the pot during firing offered by raku.

Other potters, besides Soldner, were involved in the early development of the post-firing process in raku.

Hal Riegger and Jean Griffith. These two potters, particularly, were working in raku independently, before or at the same time as Soldner, though their impact as potters has been somewhat less. Riegger experimented with post-firing in the late 1940s, and taught a course in raku at Haystack School of Crafts, Deer Isle, Maine. This was originally reported in *Ceramics Monthly*, June, 1959. Riegger's book (see Bibliography) was the first in English on the subject and he has been very active in giving workshops. Riegger has had an initial and continuing contribution to raku as a teacher and potter.[17] Jean Griffith also has continued to work raku, and is involved in teaching at Pottery Northwest in Seattle, Washington. Soldner does not himself claim to be sole discoverer of the process and it seems likely that a number of potters found themselves thinking along similar lines at about the same time. Soldner's influence, however, seems to be dominant.

The abilities and hard work of Paul Soldner and others has been mainly instrumental in creating an acceptance of raku as a valid branch of ceramics. Their workshops, teaching, and a recognizable body of work helped to disseminate raku methods, and there has developed through these efforts an aesthetic for this ware which is independent of any attempt to imitate Japanese raku. Since 1960, raku has become very popular, and not only has become the medium of many serious potters, but has even reached weekly magazines in articles called "Backyard Ceramics."

Since the innovation of post-firing reduction, the raku process has changed much. The range of glazes has increased beyond measure. Raku has also broadened its aesthetic directions and, like most successful revivals, the revival of raku contains much that is essentially original. Above all, the intrinsic nature of the process continues to stimulate the potter's responses, and the continuity provided by a gradually evolving process has assured that the raku pots of the 1970s have genuine aesthetic connections with the simple red and black tea bowls of Chojiro, and the bright pigments of Kenzan I.

Vase #2 by Frans Wildenhain. 21" (53.3 cm) high. Stoneware, unglazed, inside blue glaze. This pot shows the ability of clay to be impressed, bent, folded, coiled, scratched, and yet still be cohesive and complete. The organic forms in this pot appear to grow out of the quieter area of clay, which, together with the overall handling of the material, makes the clay seem to grow like a plant pulsating with energy received from the ground.

2 Pottery and Perception: Mind and Medium

A distinguished Japanese potter, Mr. Kawai of Kyoto, when asked how people are to recognize good work, answered simply,"with their bodies".

Bernard Leach
A Potter's Book

In his work, a potter will perpetually confront the primary material of clay—in its wet state, an amorphous, plastic substance. The potter will make a shape from it, and fix that shape, also creating texture and color according to his desire. He may be both passive and active. He may respond and impose. He may cooperate with the medium and at the same time he may bring something to it. What the potter brings will be the accumulation of his particular skill, experience, and perception. His perception will be exercised not only in the actual handling of the material, but also in the experiencing of objects he did not create, whether natural or manmade. The sharpening of perception is a lifelong task.

The word "perception" not only means the physical use of one's senses, but also denotes a mental operation involving intuition or instinct, conceptualizing and naming. We will deal with both meanings in this chapter, for both processes can help the potter. Let us begin with the physical meaning, which we will call "sense response."

Sense Response

With sense response we respond to an object's physical presence, and there is probably a stage in our perception when we do not interpret these sense responses in the slightest. The object is red, it is round, it is soft. That is all. Most of us tend to conceptualize, perhaps too much, or too fast. Very often we look at a certain assemblage of colors, textures, and form, and immediately recognize it as "cup." As "cup," this object has so much in common with other objects that serve the same function that its individuality is lost to us in favor of its conformity. This classifying and naming of things often saves time and trouble, but it also has disadvantages for the potter/observer because the habit of classification can override his

sense of what the object is. Developing your sense responses should lead to making better pots. You can sharpen your sense responses not only in the handling of the material, but in considering the pot itself—its form, its texture, and its color—and also in the contemplation of any object which presents itself to the senses.

You must have a direct perception of what is really there, and, with pots, must avoid the traps of social standards, present taste, "in" things, historic importance, even fashionable theories. This has been expressed before in different ways: Soetsu Yanagi has said that one should not interpose the intellect between one's sense responses and an object; Keats said that a sense of beauty overcomes every other consideration, or indeed obliterates all consideration.

Raku is associated from its beginning with fulfillment through direct perception. Its emergence in 17th century Japan coincided with various social and aesthetic developments—a rejection of taste in the social sense, an integration of Zen philosophy into everyday life, a stipulation that in life and in art, as well as through life and through art, one should experience directly. The word "raku" itself—meaning "pleasure," "enjoyment," or even "ease" and "comfort"—attains its true importance in this context.

Japanese raku pottery was a result of an openness to nature and natural forms. It resulted from a Zen pursuit—to perceive the oneness of the individual and the rest of creation, in fact to eradicate the sense of "otherness," and through pottery to re-create a natural object to exemplify and intensify this oneness.

For a Westerner who knows little about Zen, an honesty and directness of sense response is all that is necessary to begin working in raku. To begin with a philosophic standpoint is in some ways a disadvantage. A

Raku Suncup *by Susan and Steven Kemenyffy. Approximately 4" (10.2 cm) high. Although a cup, this* **Suncup** *does not conform to preconceptions of what a cup should be, but takes its life from landscape and sunshine.*

Raku Basket *by Howard Yana-Shapiro. The directness of handling is evident here, reflecting a philosophical as well as a physical response to the medium.*

philosophy must be arrived at through a direct involvement with the materials and the process.

The following example illustrates the benefits of simply paying attention to one's senses. Probably you have an old teacup of your grandmother's lying around. You may classify it in any number of ways: old, worn, out of date and therefore unworthy of attention; antique and worth money; historically a perfect example of a certain period or style; of great sentimental value and part of a long family history. These kinds of classifications are precisely what should be avoided. Examine this old cup for itself. Determine its individuality, which has been obscured by years of association and familiarity. Observe the form, the glaze, which give the cup its character. Realize the possibilities; try not to limit your responses to conceptual pigeon holes. This cup becomes more than just "cup"; it is a unique conjunction of color, texture, and form, and you may like it or not as such. In *A Potter's Book*, Bernard Leach writes: "Judgement in art cannot be other than intuitive and founded upon sense experience, on what Kawai calls 'the body.' No process of reasoning can be a substitute for or widen the range of our intuitive knowledge."

Natural Forms

What, then, is the beginning of a pot? Does it begin with an idea? When you touch the clay? From another pot? It would be foolish to dogmatize about where the creative act begins, but a heightened sense response will be a starting point of a kind. Furthermore, an awareness of your sense responses at every stage of creativity is probably as sure a recipe for good pots as can be given, and it is at least safe to say that you should attempt always to be open to possibilities from this source.

Many artists have acknowledged the fundamental importance of nature in their work, and some have identified their creativity with the organic principle in nature. Hans Arp, for example, writes:

Art is a fruit that grows in man, like the fruit of a plant, or a child in its mother's womb. . . . Reason tells man to stand above nature and to be the measure of all things, thus man thinks he is able to live and create against the laws of nature and creates abortions.

Originally, a raku pot was seen as an object created according to the laws of nature, raku evolving as it did because of the preference of the tea masters for natural things. For many reasons, then, it seems appropriate to seek the origin of some of your pots in your sense responses to what Goethe called "nature's open secret." Nature is not, of course, the only source for ideas, and the romantic treatment of nature has the disadvantage at present of being mistaken for mawkish sentimentality or adherence to a fad. We do not feel that inspiration from nature need produce either, and propose to use this source as an example of the benefit of sense responses. Ultimately, however, the potter may find his inspiration

Shell Plate by Richard Hirsch. Approximately 23" (58.4 cm) in diameter. 1972. Raku, partially glazed in iridescent blue and gray. Depending on how you see it, the depth of the iridescent glaze on this plate gives the feeling of the inside of a shell or the sloping sea.

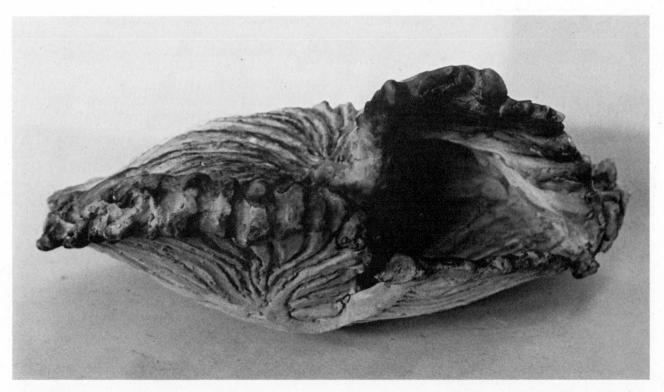

Clay Nautilus by Sister Celeste Mary Bourke. 24" (61 cm) long. Raku with engobes. A different shell with a different feeling.

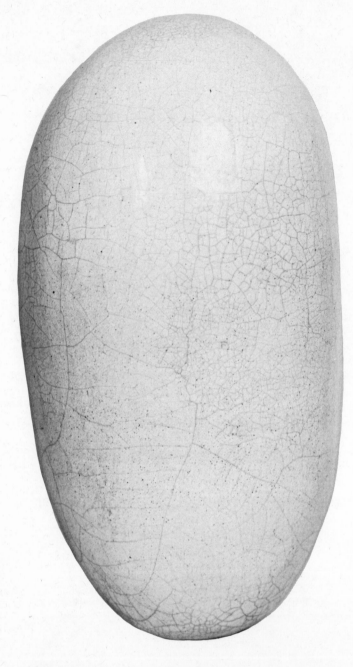

Egg-Form Vase by Richard Hirsch. 23″ (58.4 cm) high. 1974. *Raku, white crackle glaze. The scale of this pot alters the effect of the form, despite its evident source.*

in a steel mill as easily as in a meadow: it depends on an openess of mind and on what the potter/observer responds to.

Perhaps a good place for the potter/observer to start looking is with objects that are small enough to be handled. Also intersting are forms seemingly devoid of texture or color. For example, an egg when turned in the hands can be realized as a form, not just as an inert two-dimensional shape. We write later of "the inevitable occupation of space" which marks a good pot; the same inevitability applies to an ordinary egg.

Other natural shapes can be explored for their individual forms—their character. For example, rocks, beach pebbles, cliff faces, and rock crystals are basically the same material, but each offers a widely different statement of form. Water, too, is a material that takes many forms, depending on its state. Indeed, a lake or ocean offers continually changing forms to the eye while you watch. And think of water, too, in the form of icicles, snowdrifts, a raindrop. Equally rewarding in this regard are clouds and trees. Although they have the common characteristics of their general class, dependent on the material of which they are made and the forces acting upon them, both clouds and trees can be seen in an infinite range of forms.

It is possible to combine all these objects into a "landscape," which, though a collection of separate objects, nevertheless may take on the identity of a single object with a total form.

Texture

Texture is both tactile and visual and applies to surface qualities. What we call the "texture" of an object is not only what a surface feels like, but what it *looks* as though it *should* feel like. Velvet, for example, *looks* soft and *feels* soft. Sometimes the visual and the tactile match, and sometimes they do not: clouds, for example, look more solid than they are. An essential part of the aesthetic of raku pottery is the rightness of the correlation of sight and touch.

Clay, in its plastic state being a soft material, can take on a variety of textures besides having a texture of its own. Glaze also plays an integral part in the texture of a pot. Texture can be observed in nature devoid of form and color. However, eventually it will have to be correlated with these other elements in a pot.

Looking at the egg again, it can be seen what is meant by an "eggshell" texture. Textures are very distinctive and really defy precise verbal description. It is often difficult to distinguish between surface only and the material itself. The material often determines how you will respond. For example, rocks could never really be described as "soft" because of the material of which they are made. Yet rocks can be smooth in texture and therefore appear soft, while tree bark—a much softer substance—can be rough and therefore appear hard. Some

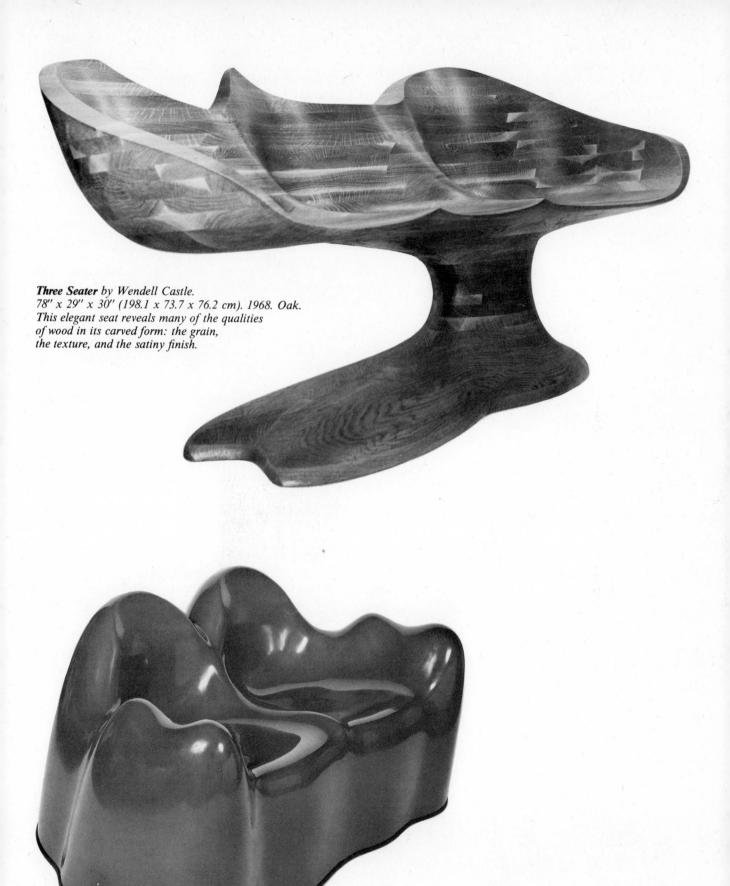

Three Seater *by Wendell Castle.*
78" x 29" x 30" (198.1 x 73.7 x 76.2 cm). 1968. Oak.
This elegant seat reveals many of the qualities
of wood in its carved form: the grain,
the texture, and the satiny finish.

Settee or Love Seat *by Wendell Castle.*
26" x 54" x 32" (66 x 137.2 x 81.3 cm). 1970. Gray fiberglass.
The choice of materials in this seat produces changes
in the design and handling of the form.

Landscape Container by Wayne Higby. 1972. Raku. The various elements in landscape here become a total form.

Hamlin Landscape 1049 (below) by Bill Stewart. Approximately 8′ x 8′ (2.4 x 2.4 m). Raku and other materials. An imaginary landscape environment reveals a different approach to the interpretation of natural forms.

Sea Heritage/A Family Album (above) by Sister Celeste Mary Bourke. 24″ (61 cm). Silk screen technique with engobes. Nature is the starting point here for an interpretation of form.

Family Album, detail.

Tea Pot by Sister Celeste Mary Bourke. 22″
(55.9 cm) high. Raku, white transparent glaze.
No attempt has been made to disguise the fact
that clay has been used to assemble this pot,
though the different uses of clay have not resulted in a lack of cohesiveness.

textures are very distinctive, like orange peel, which has given its name to the surface of a typical salt glaze.

There are many surface qualities that can be conveniently lumped under texture: matte and glossy, dull and shiny, wet and dry, coarse and fine, soft and hard, greasy, sticky, wrinkled, and many others. However, while we think it is possible to separate sensory experiences in order to examine and write about them, it is important to remember that in the process of making a pot, the textural possibilities are more often fulfilled in conjunction with the formal ones.

Color

Finally, we ask you to consider color. Most people's perception of color is so strong that the color of a pot is often what strikes the beginner before its form or texture. If a pot has a pleasing color, this has a tendency to override its other qualities. There should, however, be a correlation between form, texture, and color. In pottery, the color comes from either the clay or the glaze or a combination of the two, or from a change in these by some part of the process. Everyone knows that "Roses are red, violets are blue," but such preconceptions about color, as about everything else, can create barriers for the potter. The varieties of subtle colors are too often overlooked, and the tendency to make general classifications is especially acute in the area of color. Any object about which you have preconceptions may be reexamined to advantage for gradations in the main color, or for other colors which you may be surprised to find there at all. A change of season or of the time of day can reveal subtleties which are progressively seen as direct observation replaces preconceptions. To study color combinations, flowers both wild and cultivated are perhaps the best subjects. "Unlikely" combinations and transitions from one color to another reveal themselves in richness and abundance.

When contemplating color, you may notice more than one sensation in yourself; not only may you be absorbed in your sensuous apprehension of the color itself, but you will probably find associations crowding into your mind—associations teeming and splitting—of moods, or of particular incidents in your own life. Color is particularly apt to do this, but the same applies to form and to texture. Such subjective responses are a function of the other facet of perception; they are the active, personal elements—based on intuition and instinct—of the total process.

Candelabra by *Albert Paley.*
Iron. Attention to the properties of various media which may be both like and unlike those of clay, can reveal a lot about what clay can do. Here, the softness of heated iron reveals itself.

Squeezing.

Rolling.

The touch of hands on raw or partly formed clay is an elemental experience. Frans Wildenhain has said that, while he does not always remember in his mind all the pots he has made in a long life, his hands remember.

Intuitive Response

At the beginning of this chapter we said that perception is comprised of both sense response and intuitive response. There is more to a pot than its physical harmony of form, texture, and color, and here is where the instinctual, or intuitive, response of the craftsman/observer comes into play. The individual pot is a product of the potter's identity, but once it is made, it has a life of its own. The making of a pot requires most of the highest human qualities—patience, observation, honesty, and perseverance in the face of disappointment—and the pot will be a record of the potter's success or failure in these areas. In addition, an artist/craftsman must have—and a good pot must manifest this—an intuitive perception of the possibilities revealed by his sense responses and of the rightness of certain combinations.

The transfer of the potter's life to his pots gives life to the clay. Frans Wildenhain calls his pots his children, or, if they were made a long time ago, his grandchildren. Honesty to life through one's perceptions ultimately leads to a pot that has its own life.

Getting the Feel of the Material

The ceramic medium is earth, water, and fire. A meaningful ceramic exploits all three of these elements. In various expressions any of the three may receive more emphasis than the others.
Otto Natzler

While this part of the chapter is concerned with the primary material—clay—the process of raku as a whole is extremely important. Pots which are honestly raku in conception and execution cannot be made without experiencing this process. A beginner, for example, might conceive of and make typical stoneware pots and then fire them in a raku manner, but the result will probably not be an integrated work. Firing is particularly important to raku, as the pot is ultimately determined by what happens subsequent to its removal from the kiln. A raku firing is a continuation of the creative process, and a high degree of control must be developed.

As a beginner, it is important to understand the nature of your material, for all craftsmen have to realize the apparent limitations of their raw substances. Then, through a working knowledge of the material and the forming process, the craftsman will push his boundaries outward, and extend the apparent limitations of the medium. He begins to realize that the limitations he initially perceived in the medium were largely limitations in his skill and in his knowledge of the process. In this way, his limitations become his possibilities.

Every new student arrives encumbered with a mass of accumulated information which he must abandon before he can achieve perception and knowledge that are really his own. If he is to work in wood, for example, he must know his material thoroughly, he must have a feeling for wood. He must also understand its relation to other materials, to stone, glass and wool.[1]

Oak Table by Wendell Castle.
70″ x 19″ (177.8 x 48.3 cm). 1968.
Combining an original form and first-rate
craftsmanship, this piece functions
both as furniture and sculpture.

Doctor Jue's Bag by Marilyn Levine. 1972.
Ceramic sculpture, stoneware.
The trompe l'oeil effect of this doctor's bag
shows the versatility of clay as a material.

Lady Around by Susan and Steven Kemenyffy. 24″ (61 cm) in diameter. 1973. Raku. The form is accentuated here by the graphic element which shows both freedom in design and control of process.

Butch Cassidy by Marc Sijan. 17″ (43.2 cm) in diameter. Raku and photographic image.

Raku Basket by Nancy Jurs.
30" (76.2 cm) high. 1974.
Branch handle. Various materials
may be incorporated into a form.

In every material, there are certain natural properties. Glass, for example, before it is subjected to heat is hard and brittle, yet under the influence of heat it becomes soft and fluid. Clay, on the other hand, before it is fired is soft, yet after it is subjected to heat it becomes hard and brittle. In each medium, the natural properties of the material suggest what can be done with it; the material also imposes a timing on the craftsman, depending on what states the material goes through.

Because clay goes through various states, and in each the properties of the material at the time will be different, the craftsman must have a total conception of the process of making a raku pot and must become intimately acquainted with its properties at each stage. Eventually, the craftsman develops a rapport with his material. If, for example, a fold develops in the material and the suggestion is pleasant to the craftsman, then he may develop the work in the direction implied by the fold. The material suggests ideas to the craftsman, and he works out his ideas with the material, so that the final result is a complete cooperation between man and material.

The paradox of clay is that before firing it is a crude material—soft, squishy, very plastic, and to all appearances quite undignified. When formed and fired, it can acquire hardness and poise, and become an object of significance. In between these two states, there are certain stages which are of great technical importance to the potter because of the various properties exhibited by the material in each.

The amount of moisture in the clay determines what you can do with it. When a liquid, it is called slip and can be applied with a brush. In its plastic stage, the clay can be manipulated and does not break. It is in this stage that most of the forming takes place. Clay becomes leatherhard when most of the moisture has left the clay body, and in this stage incising, trimming, and so on, may take place without damage to the pot. When the pot has dried completely, it is known as greenware and is ready to be fired. Greenware often seems lifeless and incomplete because it is waiting for something to happen to it.

Usually, there are two firings, the bisque firing, and then, the glaze firing. It is in the glaze firing that the raku process is unique in that the ware is pulled red-hot from the kiln. Practice and familiarity with this stage is essential to the raku potter and the acquisition of skill in the firing is as important as acquiring skill with a tool.

In its finished state, a raku pot is porous and soft compared with high-fired porcelain, but marvelously rigid compared with its original plastic state. Its texture may vary according to the glaze and the clay. The properties are no longer merely properties but have become part of a totality of form and texture—the intangible spirit of the pot. The physical act of firing has become part of the finished article. The pot now occupies space and has properties of its own; it is an object with its own rightful existence.

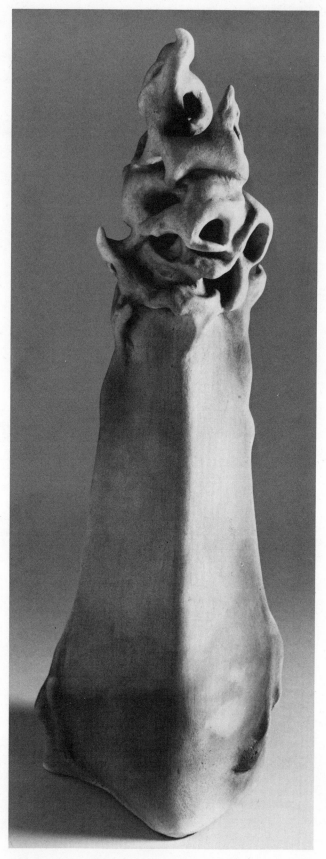

Raku Form by Marguerite Antell. 32″ (81.3 cm) high. 1974. Partially glazed. An understanding of the softness and rigidity of clay characterizes this handling of the material.

Otto Natzler writes that in contemplating the process undergone by a single pot:

One begins really to understand form, to feel it. One realizes for the first time that this form in its ideal proportions, looking as natural as if it has grown from the soil, is the expression of human hands and mind—the mood of a moment caught and retained in the soft clay. The clay will harden, the fire will give it permanence, and the fleeting moment of time will have been translated into form and preserved.[2]

The paradox of softness and hardness, the tension between transience and permanence, are part of the attraction of clay, and they apply especially to the raku process.

On such a subject as this, there is no need to apologize for returning to the utter basics. Indeed, to do so is the whole point. As a beginning and an end, then, Soetsu Yanagi's advice in the *Unknown Craftsman* (see Bibliography) seems perpetually fresh:

First, put aside the desire to judge immediately; acquire the habit of just looking. Second, do not treat the object as an object for the intellect. Third, just be ready to receive passively, without interposing yourself. If you can void your mind of all intellectualisation, like a clear mirror that simply reflects, all the better.

Whatever level of craftsmanship the potter may have attained, it is probable that direct perceptual experience with, and constant reevaluation of, the material, the process, and the final result will lead to a heightened understanding of form, texture, and color that will continue to grow.

Wallpiece by Winn Burke.
Approximately 30" (76.2 cm). 1974. Raku.
There is almost no limit to the objects
that can make an impression
in clay. This piece incorporates
body casting and pressing.

Ceremonial Goblet *by Richard Hirsch. 14″ (35.6 cm) high. 1971. Raku, thrown and slab, pulled handles. Clear glaze, sprayed and smoked. Each forming method is recognizable, yet combines into a single form.*

3

Approaches to Form and Forming

In the moments of contemplation afforded by the rhythm of wedging, many potters think of the pots they are to make with the particular clay under their hands for the first time. A box, a bowl, a jar? When the clay is raku clay, rather than stoneware or porcelain, the potter is aware of thinking in terms of different forms, based partly on the expressiveness of the groggy clay turning and folding in his fingers. Also he is probably aware of the process this clay will undergo, and may think of the studied or spontaneous alterations he may make. While wedging raku clay, and at other times when thinking of forms in raku, one is aware of the need to find a proper adjustment of form to fit the demands of the material and the process.

Forming is the gradual discovery of a form, watching it grow before your eyes and feeling it in your hands; it is a process that should be as natural as leaves to a tree. Sometimes the potter may have a form clear in his mind and invent a method for achieving it. Other times he will use a certain method of forming, and the form will suggest itself out of that method. But most often the raku pot is the result of a combination of these two approaches.

The forms of the original raku are traditional, limited mainly to tea bowls and plates for the tea ceremony. They were designed to be functional and were subtle variations on a conventional theme. How different is Western raku! The modern Western potter works in the context of a great variety of traditions and frameworks. Untraditional, individual, often large in scale, modern raku pots reveal many different aesthetics, challenging the potter's assumptions about form. Unfortunately, not only does the pottery of the distant and recent past, and the wide range of knowledge available to us, provide constant stimulation, it can also breed confusion. It is impossible to adopt the values of a society that has disappeared. Yet who has not felt helpless before the exquisite perfection of united form, idea, and technique in an ancient pot? The weight of our knowledge of the past can be both a burden and an impetus. A consideration of different approaches to form existing in the past or the present, however, can sometimes help in understanding where these approaches relate to one another, and to an idea of pure form.

The Unknown Craftsman

The work of anonymous, traditional craftsmen has influenced many contemporary potters, and has been celebrated and rationalized in Sōetsu Yanagi's book, *The Unknown Craftsman* (see Bibliography). The existence of a large body of craft objects from cultures of a long tradition provides the modern potter with the corrective influence of an unselfconscious, practical approach to pots. The work of such artisans, who were often illiterate, can show the power of unconsciously accepted beliefs, untroubled by crises of value. The "crafts" movement as opposed to the "arts," has long leaned toward the view expressed by Yanagi that beauty is an inevitable outcome of ordinariness and that "only a commonplace practicality can guarantee health in something made." An appreciation of the objects so produced often requires a special effort, as the forms often seem crude or ordinary and offend our so-called civilized and refined tastes.

The World Crafts Council Show, "In Praise of Hands," held in Toronto in 1974, tackled the problem of juxtaposing the work of self-conscious artist-craftsmen with that of unselfconscious artisans. It offered a perceptual experience in what most people already knew intellectually, that the modern crafts movement has allied itself both to the aesthetic of individual self-expression and to that of complete communal integration, exemplified by

Bowl (above) from San Bartolo, Coyotepee, Mexico. Craftsman unknown. 16″ (40.6 cm) in diameter. glazed, burnished decoration, reduced in rubber tires. This bowl shows a simplicity of form and method, and a childlike quality in the decoration.

Vase by Frans Wildenhain. 24″ (61 cm) high. Stoneware, unglazed. Representative of a generation that developed sculptural pottery, Wildenhain's work sensitivity combines many forming methods.

the unknown craftsman. While the childlike state of un-selfconsciousness of the latter is not alive in our practical tradition and is impossible to re-create, many craftsmen feel the tug toward it and the desire to evolve a standard for form which involves humanistic sympathy, a knowledge of societies, and perhaps a religious humility, just as much as it involves a response to pure form. The aesthetic of "primitive" ware seems to be involved with all these things together and this source remains a well-spring of pure, cold water to refresh many modern craftsmen.

Modern, Handcrafted Ware

Much modern production pottery belongs to a relatively recent tradition, having its roots in William Morris and the Arts and Crafts movement of the 19th century. This tradition has connections with both the "primitive" functionality, dealt with above, and with a more art-conscious aesthetic. Production ware places a great deal of emphasis on the aesthetic of use—whether a pitcher is balanced and pours properly, or whether a cup is pleasant to hold and drink out of. Bernard Leach's work exemplifies this tradition, and has been enormously influential. In his book *Pioneer Pottery* (see Bibliography), Michael Cardew talks about such pottery which gains life from use:

This aspect of pottery is not always discernible to a first casual inspection; but provided it is in daily use it will gradually become visible, just as a good character comes to be appreciated only through continued acquaintance. Its presence will fill the gaps between sips of tea or coffee at those moments when the mind, not yet focused on activity, is still in an open and receptive state; and it will minister quietly to the background of consciousness with a friendly warmth, even perhaps on some occasions with a kind of consolation.

Most of the early craft schools in America, such as Alfred and S.A.C. (School for American Craftsmen) stressed this high level of craftsmanship and functionality. Pottery of this sort has probably reached a state of perfection and its forms, besides being functionally excellent, are also made with sculptural criteria in mind—they are balanced to the eye, the volume they contain is pleasing, and the volume they displace is also considered. The glazes also work functionally and aesthetically. In such pots, however, the balance of functional and sculptural criteria are approximately equal: while functional, the ware is also the product of a self-conscious, trained mind.

Sculptural Pottery. Coexisting in the West now with the more traditional functional pottery, and having in some cases much in common with it, is the kind of pottery which could be termed "sculptural." What distinguishes it from functional ware is that the sculptural qualities predominate; indeed, many such pieces are only quasi-functional. Very often, however, this quasi-functional element remains as an important skeletal idea for the form, and many contemporary pots fit nominally into the functional categories such as vase, box, or bowl. Almost

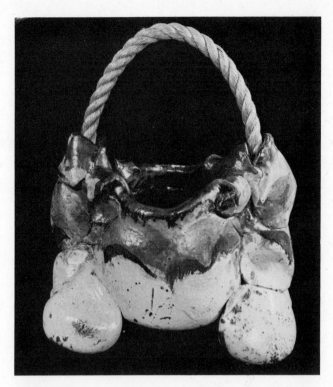

Basket by Nancy Jurs. 20" (50.8 cm) high. Rope handle. A different basket with a different sculptural quality.

Gold Luster Raku Teapot by Kit-Yin Tieng Snyder. 8" x 8" x 11" (20.3 x 20.3 x 27.9 cm). c. 1970. Starting with a functional idea, the potter has made an object which is predominantly sculptural, although it could still function as a teapot.

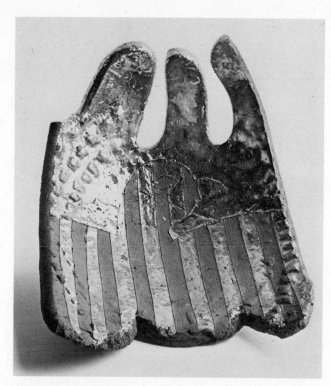

Plate *by Henry Gernhardt. 11″ x 7″ (27.9 x 17.8 cm). Silver luster and black. The major emphasis here is not on the functionality of a plate, but in sculpting and painting in the ceramic medium.*

Basket *by Betty Woodman. Partially glazed. A soft, sculptural form that retains some functional identity.*

always, pots in this category are vessels or containers of one kind or another, though they may never be used as such. The vestigial function seems to collect and focus the sculptural qualities in the form. The idea of making a "vessel" which is not intended for use represents yet another approach to form. This has been one of the major directions in ceramics since the 1950s, and is heavily represented in this book.

Sculpture in Clay. The Abstract Expressionist movement of the 1950s encouraged some potters to move from pottery which was merely sculptural towards pure sculpture in clay. The number of potters who produce sculpture in clay, rather than vessels which are *sculptural*, is still quite small, even though a strong trend suggests that, in a few years, much more ceramics may move away from sculptural vessels. The approach to form suggested by pure sculpture is already well explored in other media and requires, of course, no function. Little need be said about it here, except to emphasize the direct approach to pure form that it involves.

The area of pure sculpture is one in which raku has yet to establish itself. Originally, there were technical problems which prevented raku from attaining the size that is usually associated with sculpture. These have largely been solved. This fact, and the strength of the ordinary raku body, might suggest that the particular qualities afforded by raku will be seen increasingly in sculpture. However, insofar as some sculpture is exhibited outdoors, raku does have drawbacks. Because it is porous, the glazes can peel off the body if the piece is left outside, and frost may crack the absorbent body in winter. And because it is low-fired, the raku piece lacks structural strength. Also to be considered is the question of scale in raku, discussed later in this chapter. However, there is every reason to suppose that raku sculpture exhibited indoors will become more common now that certain technical problems have been solved.

Conceptual Approaches

Probably any piece of pottery that gains the major part of its effect by *meaning*, rather than *being*, would fit into the conceptual category. To put it another way, the person responding to this kind of pot must recognize certain symbolic elements in the piece, or must supply them out of his own knowledge. Some pots in this category may still evince a concern for the handling of the material and require a sensuous response from the person viewing the pot; on the other hand, they may require so much of a conceptual understanding that they are practically antiform. Much "funk" would serve as an example of this, where references may be specific and/or universal—from gaudy clay animals to machines with futile or uninvented functions. A lot of funk gains its strength from a satiric, or more rarely, a philosophic statement about the modern world. Many such statements seem to express Einstein's

Carolina Winter Landscape Plate *by Wayne Higby. 16 1/2″ x 18″ (41.9 x 45.7 cm). 1973. Raku, earthenware. The idea of form and the concept of a plate's function are secondary to the landscape image.*

Raku Floor Piece (above) by Susan and Steven Kemenyffy. Approximately 12′ x 12′ (3.7 x 3.7 m). The surface effects from the fire are secondary to the form.

Susan and Steven Kemenyffy working on a form at Naples Mill School. 1973. Often Steven makes the form and Susan the decoration.

view that "Perfection of means and confusion of goals, characterises our age." Often, the title of a funk piece is an important part of its statement.

It is not necessary that any of the concepts of form dealt with previously in this chapter would apply here, and, as such, this approach to form may require a separate kind of judgment. However, some funk manages to embody sculptural criteria as an astringent to the imagery.

Many potters make non-funk pieces that have a meaning accessible to only a few, or maybe to nobody besides the potter. The response to this kind of pot is often connected with knowledge originating immediately from the person appreciating the object, so that another person not in possession of this knowledge would be unable to perceive the meaning from the object itself. A good example of this is Paulus Berensohn's friendship bowls. He explains their genesis in his book, *Finding One's Way with Clay* (see Bibliography):

I wanted to make sets of pinch bowls that were deeply related. I wanted the same emblem or symbol to appear on each bowl, not as an attachment, but as if coming from the inside. And I wanted the bowls to come, as it were, from the very same ball of clay.

The knowledge that these bowls were made from the same ball of clay, more almost than the appearance that they were, becomes a moving symbolic vehicle for the act of friendship the bowls were intended to express. Again, this approach to form embodies an aesthetic where the significance of pure form is completed by other elements, and is often connected with an intellectual response to the artist's expressed intention.

The symbolic element existing in some forms is present in a different way in the original Japanese raku. The undulating rim of the tea bowl represented mountain tops, and the *cha-damari* (depression in the bottom of a tea bowl) a rain pool. Although the symbolic references in Zen are optional, and are directly perceptual as much as conceptual, this spiritual approach represents yet another alternative to pure form.

All these categories are intended to be roughly drawn. Also, they are largely theoretical and, in practice, any one pot may demonstrate elements of several categories. And, of course, other categories of form can be discovered. Hopefully, though, this brief discussion of approaches to form will serve its purpose of indicating some of the possible variations in attitudes toward the abstraction of form.

Form and Its Relationship with Other Elements

Form, however vital it is to all pots, is difficult and sometimes dangerous as an abstraction. The form of a pot is always physically involved with other elements; in fact, there may be such an interpenetration of elements that to try to separate any particular one, even abstractly, is often not possible.

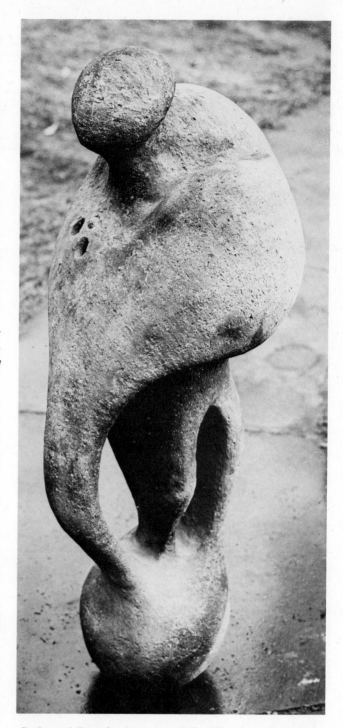

Sculptured Form *by Joan Campbell. 48" (1.2 m) high. Raku, fired and smoked in hole-in-the-ground kiln. Tones of gray, white, and black markings.*

Raku Form (above left) by Joan Campbell. *This form appears to be poised between being a vessel and pure sculpture.*

Raku Form (above right) by Joan Campbell. *40'' (101.6 cm) high. Smoked in hole-in-the-ground kiln. This form clearly belongs to 20th century developments in sculpture.*

Joan Campbell, an Australian potter, in her studio.

Landscape Storage Jar by Wayne Higby. 12 1/2" x 12" (31.7 x 30.5 cm). The inlaying describes the form and becomes a decoration.

Not only are there many conceptual approaches, but there are also many technical and procedural aspects which govern the final outcome of a form. For example, whether or not the pot is to be glazed may be a decision made at the outset of the forming, or may not be made until the form is completed. Observation of the completed form may also lead to a change of heart. A satisfying form is inherently involved with many factors.

There are no all-inclusive rules for form, though some *might* be compiled to apply to a particular process. For example, those offered by Leach in *A Potter's Book* (see Bibliography) are probably among the best for wheel-thrown forms. Otto Natzler, too, addressed the following comment to thrown forms, but his observation could apply elsewhere:

Form is not just the shape of the pot. It is the manner in which that shape develops, how it originates, how it ends.[1]

The idea of a pot rising with strength and vigor from the wheelhead is probably a good guide. With other forming methods one should search for the possibilities for form inherent in the method. Coiling, for example, probably does not lend itself to the speed in vertical movement achieved by the wheel. Though the clay does rise in coiling, the pace is slower, and this process lends itself to three-dimensional asymmetry—a lateral in and out, slow swellings and thicknesses. Each forming method reveals its possibilities to the potter as he works with it.

Form and Glaze. It is sometimes hard to say what is the decoration and what the form of a pot. Sometimes the art of decorating dictates the form and sometimes the form dictates the decoration. The complexities of surface made possible by permutations of color, texture, raw or glazed areas make for great complexity and require strong resolution. Many potters resolve these elements by making either the form or the glaze the dominant element in a particular pot. There are so many approaches to the interaction of form and decoration that there are many successful solutions and also many pitfalls.

In discussing the relationship between form and glaze, it has been suggested that the form is the bones and flesh of the pot and the glaze its skin. This seems to be a satisfying statement applicable to many pots. As with the question of form and forming, the problem of glaze and glazing can be solved partly by understanding that the end product is the result of a process, that the act of glazing can leave its mark, and that a sensitive response to all parts of the process can unify the result. Just as with form, the potter can approach his glaze with a clear idea of what he wants, or can cooperate more or less with the process along the way. The resolution of form and glaze can be achieved in the same way too: by realizing that the creation of a pot is like an arrow that points both ways—either end of it can theoretically be a starting point. The potter can either begin with an idea of a form/glaze interaction, or he can allow it to evolve as a response to the process. In raku, this is a particularly important question to resolve, because the nature of the firing and post-firing process allows the potter such a variety of surface effects which have to be related to the form, often by split second decisions. The controlled resolution of the relation of surface effects to form in the best raku provides perhaps the most notable contribution of this particular medium to the field of ceramics.

Scale. The relationship of traditional functional pottery to the human body is usually considered an important element in the pot's beauty. This is true not only with respect to the comfort it provides in being used, but also more subtly in its analogy to the body—a pot has a lip, a shoulder, a belly, a foot, and so on. As a partial consequence of this, the size of a pot has been generally limited to one which humans can lift or hold comfortably. The original raku, for example, is particularly acceptable for use by people.

The kind of statement a pot makes, however, can be altered drastically by size alone. Not that sheer expansion can make a weak form strong—often this can intensify the problems. Generally speaking, though, size gives authority to a statement and seems to give the pot an independence, or an aloofness. That this is not exclusively true is obvious to anyone who has seen, for example, small Egyptian statuettes, 4″ high, which exude authority from their smallness. A pinch pot, too, expresses a close human interaction with the clay which would be broken by the creation—if it were possible—of a huge pinch pot. All in all, the size of the pot must suit the feeling, and the consideration of alternatives of scale can be a stimulating complement to inventing a form. When Paul Soldner began working in raku in 1960, he was already interested in making small, intimate pots in reaction to the contemporary trend for big stoneware pieces. By the late 1960s, though, there was a definite feeling among young potters that raku did not have to be small and fragile. They made large pots, floor pieces, sculptural objects, and in all of them scale was an important part of the statement. There is no question that the vocabulary of raku was increased enormously by this. Now, however, there is some question as to whether raku can increase in size to an unlimited extent. Such doubt is not based on the technical difficulties, for these have been solved in the past, but on the nature of the effects created by the raku process. Just as pinch pots seem properly limited in size by the process, so too do the creation of certain surface effects in raku at present limit the size of the pieces to a certain range. The effects of smoke patterns, crackle, and partial reduction patterns are more or less fixed in size and are much more significant on a small or medium-sized pot than on a large one. Beyond a certain size the form begins to dominate these surface effects, and part of the *raison d'être* of raku is lost. The sense of intimacy with the pot which is a natural outcome of the raku process can also be lost when size passes a certain point. Much contemporary raku is

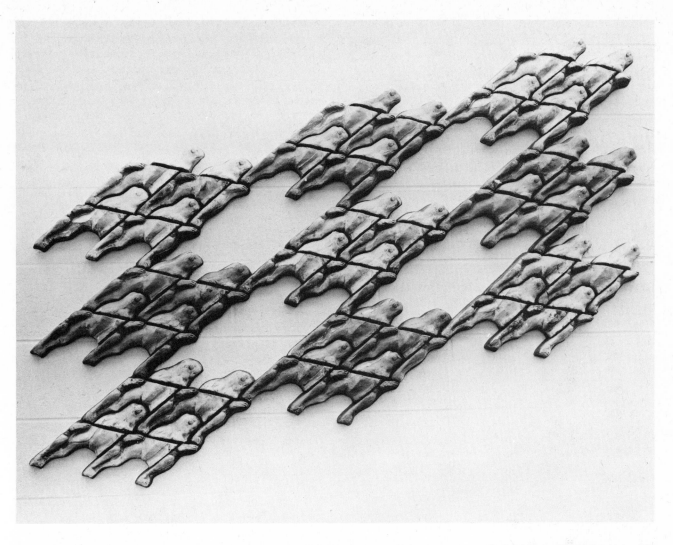

Leapin' Frog Wall *(above) by Ken Vavrek. 1974. Raku.*

Turnip *by Peter Vandengerge. 10″ x 13″ x 5″ (25.4 x 33 x 12.7 cm). Almost any form can turn up for the potter to use—and in this case he can even eat his subject afterwards!*

Hand-Over *by Winn Burke. 24" (61 cm). Raku, slab, white glaze. The title is an integral part of the piece.*

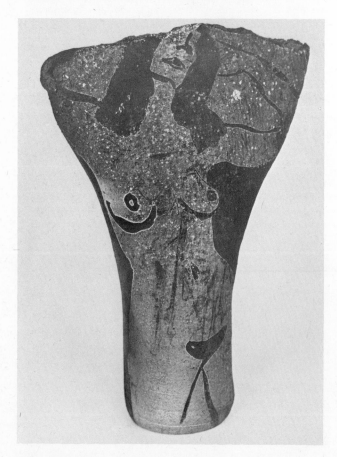

Raku Vase *by Paul Soldner. Iron and copper oxide brushed over an engobe. The contours of the decoration and form create a harmonious relationship between the two.*

still relatively small, but technically it no longer has to be so and size is now a matter of aesthetic choice. The idea of scale has already added to the technical side of raku, and has influenced the idea of raku forms. There is no reason to feel that new directions in surface effects may not be discovered in response to larger scale.

Raku Form—Is There One?

Raku, even with its many processes, seems often easily recognizable. Yet the more you think about it, the more complicated the issue of appropriate form becomes. Faced, on the one hand, with the dictum that you should respond to the process, and faced on the other with many approaches to form, can a raku form be defined at all?

Once again, one hesitates on the verge of a "rule," but raku does seem to offer a direction for form. The openness of the heavily grogged, "short" body, the direct visual contact during firing, and the spontaneous alteration during the post-firing often makes raku people feel looser, freer, than they might when working in a different medium. Raku encourages a freer handling, less readily apparent precision, and more spontaneous forms. The actual softness of the fired clay often is expressed in soft forms or in a surface treatment that suggests softness in some way. This, combined with the heritage of asymmetry and roughness in raku, often has lead both to rough, craggy forms or to raku pots which are smooth, elegant, and studied. Any answer to the question of form in raku must remain conditional: that if you can say that there is a stoneware form, a porcelain form, or an earthenware form, then you can say that there is a raku form. Each potter will hopefully find his own answer; probably it will reside in the exploitation of his particular method, his response to the medium, combined with his personal vocabulary of form.

Forming Methods

An understanding of a forming method and its particular tendencies can lead to a greater appreciation of clay, and can enrich one's concept of form itself.

Pinching. Pinching is the most basic method of making a form, requiring no tools other than the hands and giving a great deal of intimacy with the material. It was probably the method by which the original raku was formed. At one time, pinching was the forming method used out of desperation when the teacher had no equipment. It has recently been rescued as a respectable and actually very sophisticated method by Paulus Behrenson in his book *Finding One's Way With Clay* (see Bibliography). The tendency of this forming method is toward asymmetry, which agrees with a similar leaning in raku, making it a particularly suitable forming method for the process.

Throwing and Altering. The wheel has long been the standard method for rapid production. It is itself a highly

Pinching *One of the basic forming methods with clay, pinching gives the feel of the material.*

1. *A pause before beginning can allow the potter's hands and mind to adjust to the idea of pinching and help him realize the kind of form which will be shaped in his hands.*

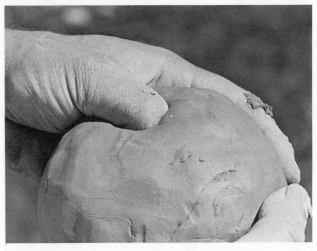

2. *The thumb thrust into the ball of clay is the first act of making a pinch pot.*

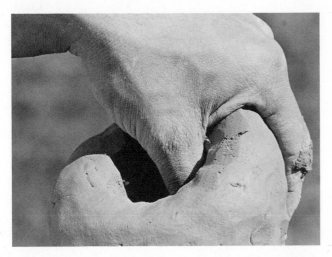

3. *The fingers on the outside and the thumb on the inside pinch, widen, and thin the walls as the vessel begins to take shape.*

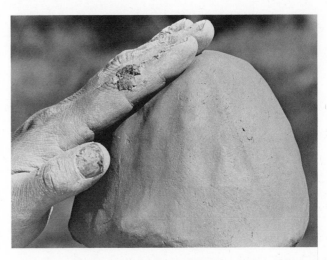

4. *Turning the pot over and working on the outside with a supporting fist inside is an optional method of developing the shape.*

5. *At this stage the process of pinching can become decoration, an integral part of the pot.*

Pinch Pot *by Richard Hirsch. 5″ (12.7 cm) high. Raku, unglazed. Pinching can lead to rhythmic, asymmetrical forms.*

Slabbing *Clay can be worked in many ways off the wheel. Its multiple properties are demonstrated here with slab techniques.*

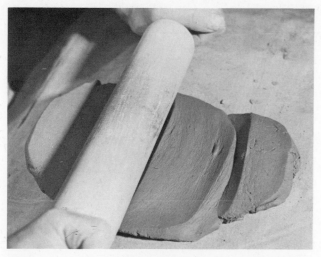

1. Slabs can be rolled out with a rolling pin—an old bottle or jar.

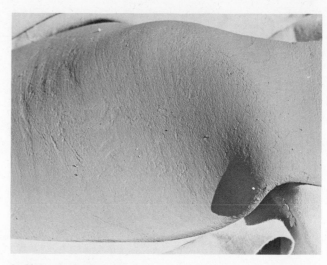

2. Slabs can be bent.

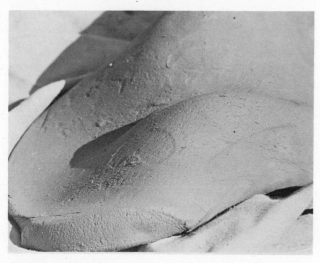

3. Slabs can be molded.

4. Slabs can be folded.

Coiling *Plastic clay can be rolled into coils which can be used for decoration on or construction of a pot.*

1. Fat or slim, coils rolled out move responsively under the hands.

2. Coils can be twisted into soft ropes.

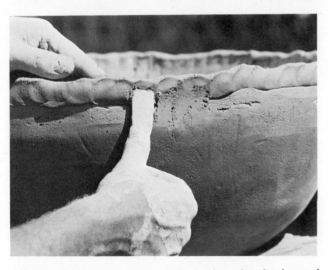

3. Coils can be added to a slabbed form, after it has dried enough to hold its shape.

4. After the coil has been applied, it can be smoothed or pinched with hands or a tool for varying effects.

Throwing *Throwing requires the use of a device other than the hands for forming the clay—a potter's wheel.*

1. *After centering the lump, the clay is opened by pressing steadily downwards with the thumbs.*

2. *Using hands locked together as one, the walls are raised by the pressure between fingers inside and outside the form.*

3. *The raising process continues, thinning out the walls and shaping the form at the same time. The bulge shows how the clay is urged to move upwards by the potter's fingers.*

4. *A continuation of refining and thinning the walls.*

Raku Pot *by Betty Woodman. 9 1/2″ x 11 1/2″ (24.1 x 29.1 cm). Thrown. While the characteristics of throwing are retained, the additions to and distortions of the form show the spirit of raku.*

Winter Tea Bowl

Tea bowls made in a traditional way are thrown, and then, unlike trimming in the Western sense, they are considerably altered when leather hard by a process which is virtually subtractive sculpture. There are 14 different tools, each designed for a specific part of the process. Howard Yana-Shapiro demonstrates the technique here which he learned while working at the raku factory in Kyoto, Japan.

1. The first stage is sculpting the foot.

2. Hollowing out the inside of the foot with a special tool.

3. Another tool is used to undercut the foot.

4. Sculpting the outer contour of the bowl while rightside up.

5. Work begins on the lip.

6. Carving is done on the inside of the lip, as well as on the undulating rim itself.

7. Carving the inside.

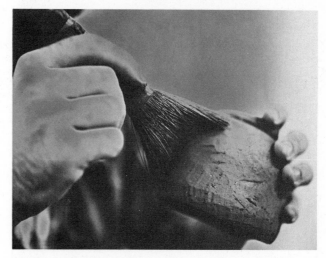

8. Brushing off the pot at the end.

Summer Tea Bowl

The processes for the summer tea bowl are in essence the same as for the winter. The warmer weather of summer allows the tea to cool more slowly, therefore, the summer tea bowl can be more open than the winter one, as the bowl itself does not have to conserve the heat of the tea. Each tea bowl is in sympathy with its season.

1. Sculpting the foot.

2. Hollowing out the inside of the foot.

3. Using a special tool to shape the inner rim of the foot.

4. Undercutting the foot.

5. Carving the outside.

6. Carving the bottom.

7. Carving the inside.

8. Brushing off the pot.

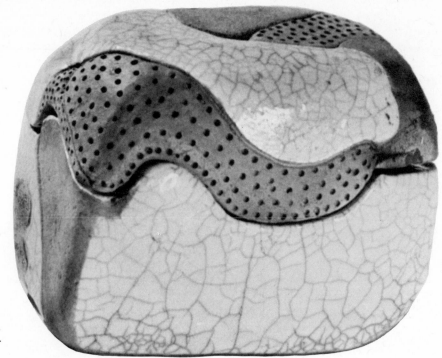

Raku Lidded Box by Nancy Baldwin. 5″ (12.7 cm) long. 1973. Slab construction; partially glazed and smoked.

Nancy Baldwin on her boxes:

I used to want my boxes to be nature-oriented or have lots of character like old people, but these ambitions are too limiting. Now I want them to BE. I want them to be clay-like, look fire-formed, live gracefully in the world, to be pleased with themselves, but humble in the knowledge that they came from clay. . . . The insides of my boxes are equally important as the outsides. . . . I carve, smooth, smoke, glaze or put collages in my boxes. The edges where inside and outside meet have a special importance too, as do corners.

Raku Lidded Box by Nancy Baldwin. 12″ x 13″ (30.5 x 33 cm). 1972. Slab construction.

sophisticated and flexible tool that lends speed and decisiveness to almost any kind of shape. It allows almost infinite modulations of outline within its strong tendency toward symmetry. Relatively recently there has been a modified use of the wheel. From what might be called the Bernard Leach tradition of stoneware forms, stressing the importance of thorough craftsmanship and exploitation of the possibilities of the wheel alone, many craftsmen now use the wheel as a tool to produce a form which is merely a starting point for further alteration. The wheel can be used to attain quickly a form which is to be added to or distorted in a combination of ways. Many potters in raku feel that this use of the wheel is the one best suited to the irregular tendencies of raku forms.

Slab. Bernard Leach refers to slab work as "a kind of ceramic joinery" and certainly one traditional use of slabs is to give a planar surface and butted corners. Slabs can also be altered to exploit the plastic nature of clay; they can be bent, wrinkled, folded, and so on. Perhaps the majority of modern raku incorporates slab construction to some extent, as the method allows great control over thickness, can tend toward asymmetry, and lends itself to the softness of surfaces and forms which characterize much raku.

Coiling. Though coiling is relatively slow, it is a traditional method in many folk-craft oriented societies. Coiling is a popular method used by many non-traditional potters for making large, asymmetrical forms. Many potters appreciate the intimacy gained with coiling that can be lost in the swiftness of the wheel. Coiling is one of the more versatile of the basic methods of forming, as the pot can be dried progressively to support the next stage of the form. Once again, the amount of control over asymmetry that this method allows causes it to be used commonly in contemporary raku.

Combinations. Of course, all these methods may be combined with one another for various reasons. The cohesive relation of methods in the finished work generally has to be considered in such cases.

Conclusions

Generally speaking, one can make no *ex cathedra* pronouncements about form and forming, without finding an obvious contradiction in the form of an excellent pot! All the approaches to form are tempered in contemporary Western ceramics with a high degree of individual self-expression, and possibly the main tradition is what has been called the "tradition of the new." We can conclude in general that form is not really an abstraction but in fact is ambiguously involved with other, equally ambiguous and equally involved, elements in the same pot. To find a raku form (to persist in talking about twin abstractions that may not really exist) involves a personal response to the medium, combined with a particular form preference that the individual potter may have. To deal with abstractions as though they really exist, as we have tried to do, might help to clarify the issue, as long as the potter's conclusions are applied concretely not just by his mind, but by his hand and heart as well.

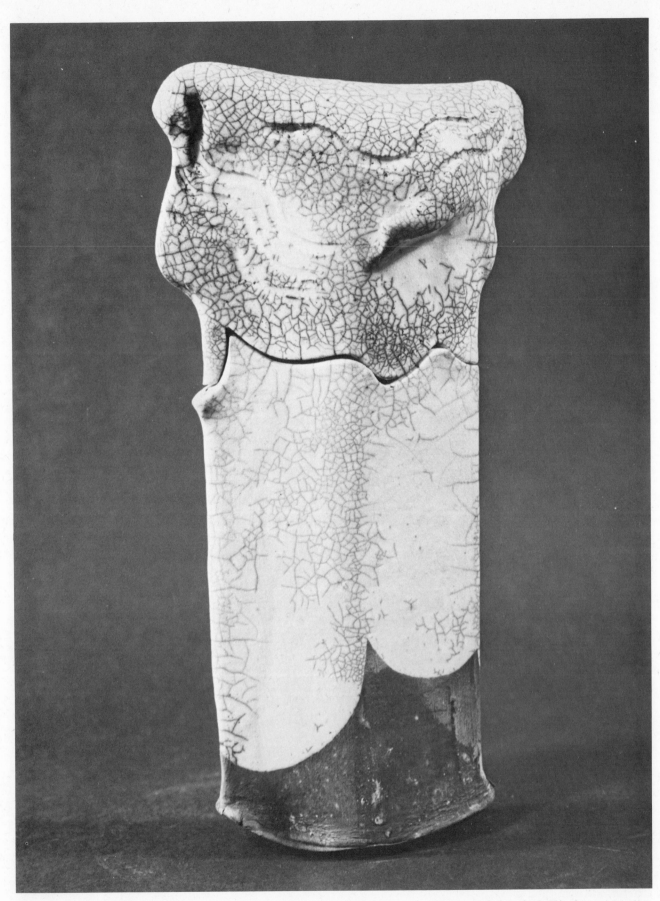

Raku Box *by Richard Hirsch. 12″ x 5″ (30.5 x 12.7 cm). 1973. Slab construction; partially glazed and smoked. The glaze pattern is a strong decorative element on the pot.*

4

Clay and Glazes

The understanding of materials, and a sensitivity to them, though it may come quicker to some people than to others, is usually a form of slow enlightenment, taking time and experience to achieve. Just as clay is a material and behaves in certain ways according to the conditions imposed upon it, so too is glaze a material: a sensitivity to it can be acquired through prolonged experience. A glaze is glass-like, it reacts to heat, and it bears the evidence of its fluidity; at its best a glaze may seem to have life, rather than being composed of inert chemicals.

One of the primary objectives in dealing with clay and glazes, in a book as well as in a pot, is to realize the complete interaction between the two materials. Raku offers many possibilities for such interaction. For example, the clay has positive characteristics of its own and its texture and color may have many affinities with those of the glaze. The smoking or post-firing in raku enlivens the clay surface, and unifies the clay and glazed areas. Generally, the unification of glazed and unglazed areas is brought about in raku as the clay darkens in post-firing and even invades the glazed areas as a crackle.

While the choice of a glaze to complete the form of the pot is obviously important, the application of glaze deserves just as much attention as the choice of glaze itself. However congenial the glaze may be to the clay form, if the glazing technique apparent in the finished pot disturbs this relationship, rather than completes it, then the pot will only jar the senses. The philosophical connection between raku and Abstract Expressionism will be discussed in Chapter 7. Here we see that raku pieces reveal the Abstract Expressionist preference for recording the energies of the process in the finished work. In this respect, the vigor of the actual glaze application may become one of the most dominant elements in a raku pot.

The Interaction of Clay and Glaze

Though an understanding of the interaction of clay and glaze is mostly obtained through experience, a few truisms on the subject may be offered here.

Forming and glazing might be thought of as parts of one process. To put it another way, bad results can come from making a form without prior thought to glazing. The more comprehensive an idea the potter has to begin with, the more unified his pot will probably be.

Knowing about the behavior of your glazes is important to their application and to the final outcome of the pots. Glaze is a liquid suspension when applied, and changes to a molten liquid while in the kiln. The fact that the final, solidified surface is the result of this change can give a potter many fruitful ideas. Glaze can melt down the rim of the pot, thinning the glaze and thereby changing the color, in some cases, as well as the texture and thickness of the skin. It melts often with the rhythm of the form, pooling in the hollows, sliding to hang in beads over the foot.

With experience, the potter gains a feeling for firing and how it changes chemicals. The idea of a finished pot can thereby be present to him as he works with raw materials: he knows what his raw clay will look like fired and smoked, and he knows what changes will be wrought by the fire on the appearance of the glaze.

The application of the glaze should be as rhythmic and natural as the firing and post-firing. This could be said about the various forming processes also, particularly throwing, but the glazing is so much quicker—often just a rapid dip, a twist, or a pour—that the speedy, rhythmic aspects are intensified. Forcing or reworking effects in glazing does not usually succeed. When glazing, it is helpful to be in a state of mind where there is speed but no hurry, decisiveness but no forcing.

The speed of a raku firing should be taken into account when glazes, glazing, and the interaction of the glaze with clay is being considered. Because a raku pot may be glazed and fired within a day, and perhaps other pots immediately undertaken which may be based on the experiments and discoveries of that pot, there is room for more trial and error in raku than is usually the case with other ceramic media. Variability and daring can become part of raku because of this speed; glazing is particularly open to spontaneity. The opportunity for many experiments in a comparatively short time allows the potter an excellent chance to work out the problems of surface, color, texture, and positioning which are the important elements in a successful relationship between clay and glaze. Spontaneity, variability and daring may be some of the unifying factors in a raku pot.

When confronted with a multitude of recipes for clays and glazes in raku, the potter is often struck by the problems of choice. There are three ways of choosing a clay body and a glaze: the potter may invent one for himself, using his knowledge of chemistry and chemicals and trial and error testing; he may look up a glaze in a book; or he may "trade" or receive a glaze formula by word of mouth from another potter. The first method can be very satisfying, but also very time consuming. The second and third, of course, are quicker but have drawbacks also. The processes which a raku clay body and glaze undergo may be so individual (indeed, that is one of the advantages of raku) that the glaze in one potter's hands may have hardly any of the properties advertised for it by the book or by the other potter. If the potter uses many clay bodies and glazes, then all of these uncertainties are multiplied. It might, therefore, be to the advantage of the potter to use one clay body and two or three glazes with which he is familiar, and which suit him with their range of effects. In this way, some of the variables in the relationships of clay and glaze can be fixed, leaving a more manageable number of problems to be investigated.

The interrelationships between clay and glaze are best understood on the spot: by making pots and closely observing and recording the results. Practice and experience, combined with some theoretical knowledge, can usually bring deeper understanding.

Clay

Clay is a natural substance derived from the weathering and decomposition of granite and feldspathic rocks. Clays can be classified according to their geological origin as being either residual or sedimentary. Residual clays are characterized by fine and coarse clay particles mixed together, relative nonplasticity, and pureness. Sedimentary clays have a finer, more homogenous particle size, are therefore more plastic, and usually contain organic matter and other mineral impurities. Because of its particular rock origin, clay mainly consists of silica

and alumina, chemically combined with water by hydrolosis. Thus the ideal formula for clay is $Al_2o_3 + 2SiO_2 + 2H_2O$, although as it is found in nature, clay usually contains many organic and nonorganic impurities. Organic impurities may affect the working properties of clay, and nonorganic impurities may affect its color and temperature range.

Probably the most unique property of clay is its plasticity. This phenomenon enables clay in its raw state to be formed and shaped by external pressure and to retain its shape once the pressure is withdrawn. Particle size and shape, along with the amount of organic matter found in a certain clay, will account for its degree of plasticity. Wet plastic clay can be formed and shaped; this unique substance when dried and sufficiently heated, becomes hard, stable, and permanent.

Clays are selected for their individual characteristics that fulfill specific requirements. Kaolins, ball clays, sagger clays, and fireclays all have their own unique properties. They may be chosen for their plasticity, color, texture, and firing range. Sometimes these requirements cannot be met by a single kind of clay. In this case several clays are mixed together along with needed earthy materials. This mixture, combination, or blend, is called a clay body. Most clay bodies are formulated to create a material that has suitable plasticity, minimal warpage and shrinkage, desired fired color and texture, glaze fit, and the needed density within a specific firing range. A clay body that is suitable for raku not only must meet those requirements but, because of the nature of the process, must resist thermal shock. When a clay vessel is rapidly heated and then quickly cooled, as in raku, tremendous physical stress is put on the clay body. The sudden expansion and contraction causes thermal shock failure, the result of which is cracking. Usually a very open, porous, nonelastic clay body will resist thermal shock failure. Earthenware clays, a low temperature (cone 08 to cone 02, 1751° to 2058° F., 945° to 1101° C.) group, can be used for raku.

Most earthenware becomes fairly hard and dense at about cone 06 (1830° F., 991° C.). Although earthenware always remains slightly porous at that temperature, it might be too dense to withstand thermal shock. If it is underfired to correct this, the results will be a clay body that has a very poor tensile strength. Because of its natural properties, if fired too high most earthenware will deform by blistering and bloating around cone 1 (2100° F., 1149° C.). This is still within the raku firing temperature. Therefore stoneware clays—those which mature at a much higher temperature range—are usually selected, ingredients being added to them to meet the specific requirements of raku. Sufficient amounts of sand or grog (between 10% and 30%) added to stoneware clay will help open up a clay body and make it more porous. This will cut down shrinkage in drying and aid in resisting thermal shock during the firing and post-firing. Other ingredients can be added to make the raku clay body less

Second Plant Man
by Susan and Steven Kemenyffy.
Approximately 48″ (121.9 cm) high.
Covered jar with luster and fumed decoration.
Technically complicated,
the decoration uses glazes, underglazes,
and fuming, yet it combines with a form
which is strong enough to support
the visual complexity.

Only Island #1 by Ken Vavrek. 1973. Thrown and hand built.

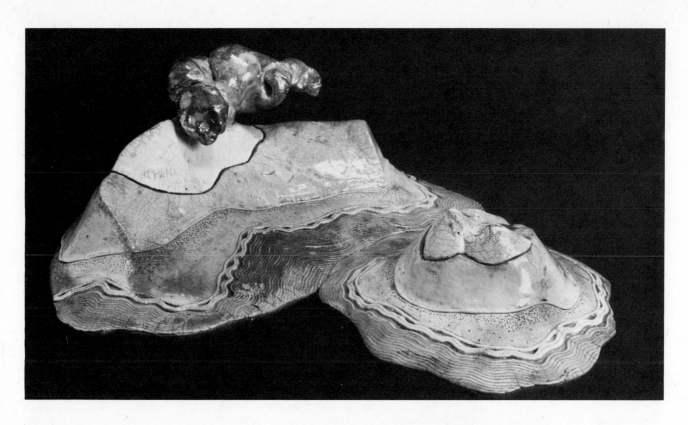

Winter Beach—Landscape Containing 30 Gold Moon Snails (above) by Wayne Higby. 20" x 24" x 18" (50.8 x 61 x 45.7 cm). 1972. Raku, earthenware. Control of the glaze application and of the effects of post-firing characterizes much of Higby's work.

Triangle Springs—Landscape Container by Wayne Higby. 7" x 10" (17.8 x 25.4 cm). 1973.

elastic and thus more resistant to expansion and contraction. Petalite and spodumene, both lithia compounds, reduce thermal expansion and can be used to increase shock resistance for raku clay bodies. Talc is a commonly used ingredient in raku bodies. Along with adding to the tensile strength of the clay at low temperatures it also helps to reduce heat shock.

As a general rule, raku clay bodies contain between 20% and 40% non-clay, nonplastic materials that resist heat shock, using various combinations of sand, grog, petalite, spodumene, talc, flint, feldspar, vermiculite, pearlite, wollastonite and others. Most often there are three types of clays that are incorporated into a raku clay formula. Since most raku clay bodies are stoneware, a general-purpose stoneware clay is used as the base of the raku body. Stoneware clays such as Cedar Heights Goldart and Jordan work well and are suitably plastic. Fireclay, a refractory, stoneware type of clay, is added to give a coarse texture, or "tooth," which also helps keep the body open and porous. Most fireclays are not very plastic, therefore some ball clay is required to make the body plastic and workable.

In fact, almost any clay will work. A natural, locally found earthenware or stoneware clay can be made shock resistant and workable by opening it up with sufficient additions of fireclay and sand or grog.

Probably the most important factor in the success of a raku clay body is the temperature of the bisque. Ideally, the bisque temperature should render the clay body sufficiently open, porous, underfired, yet with enough tensile strength so that it can easily be handled. The exact firing temperature of the bisque ware, then, depends on the type of clay body you are working with (basically either earthenware or stoneware), and the specific requirements of the clay vessels you expect to make and their glazes. Following is a group of raku clay bodies given in parts by weight.

White Raku

Missouri fireclay	25
Cedar Heights Goldart	30
Tennessee #5 ball clay	15
Spodumene	5
Grog (fine mesh)	20

White Raku (from Ken Vavrek)

Missouri fireclay	50
Ball clay	50
F-1 wollastonite	15
Mullite (35 mesh)	15
Talc	10
Grog	10

White Raku (from Adele Zimmerman)

Missouri fireclay	50
Old Mine #4 ball clay	30
Medium grog	20

White Raku (from Dave Tell)*

Fireclay	50
Stoneware clay	20
Ball clay	25
Talc	5
Sand	50

Brown Raku (from Dave Tell)*

Fireclay	50
Stoneware clay	20
Cedar Heights Redart	25
Talc	5
Sand	50

*DuPont shredded nylon (see Suppliers List for where to obtain this) can be added into the mix and acts like chopped fiberglass for dry strength but the nylon doesn't cut your hands.

White Raku

Plastic fireclay	50
Talc	20
Sand (30 mesh)	30

Buff Raku

PBX fireclay	30
Jordan clay	15
Ball clay	25
Cedar Heights Goldart	15
Grog	15

White Raku

North American fireclay	50
Cedar Heights Goldart	50
Grog (28 mesh)	30

Buff Raku

Cedar Heights Goldart	30
PBX fireclay	25
Calvert clay	15
Buckingham feldspar	10
Flint	10
Grog	25

White Raku

Missouri fireclay	50
Ball clay	30
Talc	20
Grog	20

White Raku

North American fireclay	40
Tennessee #5 ball clay	20
Kentucky Special ball clay	10
Grog	20
Spodumene	10

Raku Body (from Nancy Baldwin)

Cedar Heights Goldart	100 lbs.
Screened garden soil	⅓ bucket
Screened beach sand	⅓ bucket

Glazes

Most raku glazes fall into the low temperature range—roughly 1458° to 2048°F. (764° to 1101°C.). Identification of the two major categories in this firing range is according to the most important flux in the glaze composition. A flux, to put it simply, is a melting ingredient which influences the other chemicals in the glaze to melt. In the low temperature range, the two major groups are divided into lead-based glazes and alkaline-based glazes.

These different base glazes, however, share many common characteristics, some of these being evident in raku. Despite the relatively low temperature, raku glazes composed of either of these bases melt and flow easily, usually into a smooth, glassy surface. Especially evident in raku is the tendency for low-fire glazes to craze. Crazing is caused by a different rate of contraction between the glaze skin and the clay body during cooling. Because raku ware often undergoes rapid expansion and contraction in the firing, and in the smoking procedure of post-firing, the pattern from crazing is a major characteristic of raku glazes. When this glaze "flaw" is used in a decorative manner, it is known as a crackle glaze.

Low-fire glazes also have, as a general characteristic, the ability to produce a wide color range. Bright colors are usually obtained from the standard coloring oxides of cobalt, iron, copper, and others. Usually, these colors are intense and uniform. Because of the low temperature range, these glazes are not as subtle as in high-fire stoneware, where the colors are muted by the intense heat and often by the atmospheric conditions.

With low temperature ware, it is relatively clear in a cross-sectional view of the pot where the glaze ends and the clay begins. Although fusion between the two layers does take place, it does not take place to the great extent of porcelain or high-fire stoneware, where it is much more difficult to tell where one layer ends and the other

begins. Therefore, in raku, little chemical or physical interaction between glaze and clay takes place.

Oxidation and Reduction. At this point in any general discussion about glazes, and especially about raku glazes, it is necessary to mention the two most common atmospheric conditions in the field of pottery, oxidation and reduction. Oxidation and reduction affect the surface quality of the glaze, its color, and even the color of the clay.

An oxidation atmosphere, simply speaking, is one that has plenty of oxygen and is relatively free of carbon. In this atmosphere the melted, fused chemicals on the pot in the kiln will all be in their oxide form, because they have combined with the plentiful oxygen. In a reduction or reducing atmosphere, however, significant amounts of carbon or carbon monoxide are present. Both free carbon and carbon monoxide have a great affinity for oxygen and easily combine with the oxygen from the oxides in the glaze chemicals. Certain ceramic chemicals, when deprived of their oxygen content, are said to be reduced. Reduction can have a major effect on the color of the coloring chemical. For example, copper oxide in its melted oxidized form is usually green. When it is deprived of its oxygen in a reducing atmosphere, it can be shades of red and even be reduced to its metallic color, like a new copper penny.

Reduction can also change the surface quality of the glaze and the color of the clay body. In the post-firing of raku, the hot clay is typically subjected to a heavy reducing atmosphere containing free carbon from burning combustibles. This carbon is deposited on the surface and can turn a white clay anywhere from gray to jet black.

Lead Glazes

It is surprising that even today when so much is known about the toxicity of lead that so many studio potters still use it. In some European countries and in Mexico, lead is still widely used in some pottery industries. Perhaps the overriding reason is that the qualities and characteristics of lead glazes cannot be duplicated with any other glaze materials.

Until a few years ago, all raku glazes were thought to require some lead compounds, probably because lead-base glazes were used traditionally for raku ware. This originated with Chojiro's using a lead-based glaze on all his raku except the black. Lead was the major ingredient in the raku formulas used by Ogata Kenzan I and Koetsu that were eventually handed down to Tomimoto and Bernard Leach. In his *A Potter's Book*, Leach gives some of these traditional formulas:

Clear Base

White lead	66
Quartz	30
China clay	4

Raku Vessel *by Richard Hirsch. 26" (66 cm) high. Thrown, slabbed with pulled handles. The glaze application relates to the roundness of the handles and the belly of the pot.*

Raku Vase by Joan Campbell. 24" (61 cm) high. Soft brown,
white, and green glazes. The unique textural quality of this piece
is due to the addition of mica to the clay body.

Clear Base

White lead	61
Frit	18
Impure silica	21

At the time these were perhaps the only raku glaze formulas known in the West. When Paul Soldner first experimented with raku, the initial glazes he used were lead
based.

Advantages of Lead Glazes. Lead is the most powerful
flux for low-temperature firing. Lead glazes melt and
flow easily and usually produce a smooth, shiny, reflective surface, so that it is easy to tell by eye when they are
melted. Though lead melts by itself at about 950°F.
(510°C.), in a glaze its firing range without volatization is
usually between cone 016 to cone 02 (or 1458° to 2048°F.,
764° to 1101°C.).

Usually the coloring oxides in a lead-base glaze produce a wide range of intense, bright colors which are generally predictable and uniform. For example, cobalt will
give blues; iron, tans and browns; copper, greens in oxidation; and manganese, brown-purple.

Disadvantages of Lead. Lead's most serious disadvantage
is, of course, that it is poisonous. It is extremely toxic both
in its raw state, and after it has been melted. Lead can be
ingested both from direct contact in handling or from
breathing in the raw dust.

Lead is not only dangerous to the potter; it is also dangerous to the user. Even after having been melted, lead is
soluble. The large amounts of lead in a traditional raku
glaze can be dissolved in the weak acids often present in
food and drink, and therefore be poisonous to the user.

To avoid the hazard of toxicity in the raw state, lead
can be introduced into the base glaze as a frit. A lead frit
is usually a complete glaze that has been melted and
ground into a powder to avoid the toxic effects of raw
lead. Even in this form, however, there remains the possibility that the lead contained in this glaze may still be
slightly soluble when melted. To be perfectly safe, therefore, the use of lead should be restricted to nonfunctional
ware. For functional ware, glazes with a base other than
lead should be used.

A less damaging defect of lead-based glazes, though
important enough to the potter, is that these glazes do not
react well to a reduction atmosphere inside the kiln. They
may bubble and blister with ugly results. Following is a
group of lead compounds.

Lead Carbonate ($2PbCO_2 . Pb(OH)_2$). Lead carbonate is
a white powder whose common name is white lead. This
lead material is most often the form used in traditional
raku formulas; it is easy to apply to bisque ware and usually has few flaws when melted.

Lead Monoxide (Pb_3O_4). Lead monoxide, commonly
called "red lead" is also in common use in raku.

Lead Silicate and Lead Monosilicate. These are being used more often now by studio potters because they are combinations of lead fritted with silica. This practice eliminates the toxic effects of lead in the raw state.

Lead and Lead Frit Glazes

In general, frits are prepared by melting lead or the soluble alkalies of potash or soda and also boric oxide with more stable, less soluble chemcials. After they are fused together the entire new compound is quickly quenched and ground into a fine powder. Frits are thus total glazes in themselves and have certain properties and compositions. Some lead frits are: Ferro—3304, 3377, 3396, 3403, 3379, 3419 and Pemco—P545, P658.

Extreme care should be taken when mixing and using these glazes. Lead is toxic in its raw state as well as when it is melted. Lead frits, while not toxic to handle in powder form, may have some lead solubility when they are melted. Users of vessels with these glazes should be cautioned. Following is a group of lead and lead frit glazes given in parts by weight.

Base

White lead	50
Borax	10
Kaolin	2
Flint	40

Clear

White lead	60
Colemanite	25

Base

White lead	60
Frit 3124	20
Flint	20

White

White lead	60
Flint	20
Frit P25	20
Tin oxide	3

White

Colemanite	70
Buckingham feldspar	15
Red lead	10
Kaolin	5

Off White

White lead	60
Frit 3124	20
Flint	20
Tin oxide	1

Raku by Betty Woodman. The glaze application is a dominant factor in this pot.

Raku Form *by Richard Hirsch. 14″ (35.6 cm) high. 1974. Thrown and coiled, glazed, sprayed, and smoked.*

Silver White

White lead	50
Frit 3110	30
Flint	15
Nepheline syenite	5

Orange

White lead	60
Frit P25	40
Lead chromate	4

Orange–Red

White lead	77
Borax	9
Flint	14
Chrome oxide	0.3

Orange

Red lead	229
Kaolin	25.8
Flint	30
Chrome oxide	7.6

Orange (from Nancy Baldwin)

Red lead	300
Frit 3304	200
Flint	15
Kaolin	15
Green chrome oxide	6

Yellow

White lead	40
Kaolin (EPK)	5
Flint	10
Soda ash	5
Frit 3110	40
Lead chromate	3

Yellow

White lead	48
Frit 3124	16
Flint	16
Tin oxide	8
Lead chromate	8

Light Green

White lead	60
Frit 3110	20
Flint	20
Copper carbonate	3

Black Luster

White lead	60
Frit 3403	20
Flint	20

Add to base:

Copper oxide	4
Cobalt oxide	3
Iron oxide	4

Black

White lead	60
Flint	40
Frit 529	20

Add to base:

Cobalt oxide	2.5
Red iron oxide	4
Copper oxide	2

Base (from Dave Tell)

Lead frit	80
Kaolin (EPK)	10
Gerstley borate	5
Borax	5

Base

Frit 3396	80
Kaolin	5
Borax	10
Gerstley borate	5

Base

Frit 3403	75
Feldspar	20
Ball clay	5

Base

Frit 529	70
Gerstley borate	5
Flint	10
Soda ash	10
Kaolin	5

Alkaline Glazes

Alkaline glazes comprise the other major category, besides lead, in the low-temperature range. Although not used traditionally in Japan, these glazes at present are widely used and accepted in contemporary raku. That they are safe and produce good results is probably an important reason for their popularity. In addition, they are

Raku Vase *by Paul Soldner. Engobes and stains. Simplicity of form is enhanced by free, calligraphic glaze application.*

predictable, offer a wide range of surface qualities, often produce beautiful colors, and melt within the usual raku temperature range.

Alkaline-type glazes rely on the strong fluxing power of the alkalies of potassium, sodium, and lithium. These active fluxes produce glazes that are soft, fluid, and glassy. While some degree of crazing is almost always present, this can be used to advantage in raku.

Many chemicals are used as the source of these alkaline fluxes. Some of them, however, have intrinsic drawbacks. For example, alkaline glazes rely on some chemicals that are soluble in water, i.e., that dissolve in it. This can cause problems in application, storage, and even in the melted layer of glaze. If, for example, too much soluble material from the raw glaze is absorbed by the porous bisque ware, an uneven, rough, incomplete glaze might result on the fired ware.

Some soluble materials containing alkalies are hygroscopic, i.e., they absorb moisture and become lumpy and difficult to mix into the raw glaze batch. Another problem with hygroscopic chemicals is that calculation by weight is difficult owing to the uncertainty of the amount of water absorbed. Two of the most common chemicals which have the complicating (in this case) properties of being hygroscopic and soluble are soda ash or sodium carbonate ($Na_2.CO_3$) and borax ($Na_2O.2B_2O_3.10H_2O$).

Borax contains significant amounts of boric oxide and is the strongest flux other than lead in the low temperature range. Boric oxide, although normally listed with the silicas because it is a glass former, is a very powerful flux and produces strong colors similar to those more conventionally classed as alkaline fluxes. Like most substances that contain large amounts of alkalies, boric oxides are soluble. Of these, colemanite ($2CaO.3B_2O_3.?5H_2O$) has the advantage of being only slightly soluble. It is the only natural substance containing boric oxide with this property, therefore it is in constant demand. Colemanite may, in fact, be difficult to obtain but substitutes can be made. Gerstley borate is a synthetic colemanite that is similar to, yet not quite the same as, its natural counterpart. When substituting Gertsley borate for colemanite, use about 25% more Gerstley borate. The only other way to introduce boric oxide into a glaze without the fear of solubility is with a frit.

Frits have the advantage of rendering the alkaline fluxes insoluble, thereby eliminating all the problems of solubility. Another advantage is that formulas containing fritted material simplify glaze calculation because of the combination of many needed chemicals into one material. Because frits have already been melted once, less boiling and volatilizing takes place, and the glaze quickly develops a smooth, even melt during the short raku firing cycle.

Some leadless alkaline frits containing boron commonly used in raku glazes are: Ferro—3230, 3110, 3124,

3134, 3191, 3195, 3211; Pemco—P-54, P-25, P-238.

Feldspar is the most common insoluble source of the alkalies of sodium and potassium. Feldspar is usually divided into two categories as being either soda feldspar ($Na_2O.Al_2O_3.6SiO_2$) or potash feldspar ($K_2O.Al_2O_3.6SiO_2$). Unfortunately, large amounts of feldspar cannot be used within the low temperature range of raku, because the large amounts of alumina and silica make it refractory at low temperatures. Following is a group of low temperature alkaline and boron glazes given in parts by weight.

Clear Base (from Adele Zimmerman)

Frit 3134	70
Borax	10
Colemanite	20

Clear Base (from Nancy Baldwin)

Frit 3110	80
Borax	10
Kaolin	5
Gerstley borate	5

Clear Base (from Ken Vavrek)

Frit G-14	50
Nepheline syenite	15
Colemanite	15
Ball clay	10
Frit 3191	5
Barium carbonate	5

Clear Base

Frit P-25	43.6
Frit 3134	26.3
Lithium carbonate	9.9
Kaolin	10.2
Flint	14

White

Colemanite (or Frit W-15)	90
Ball clay	10
Cornwall stone	10

White

Frit P-25	36
Frit 3134	28
Kaolin	8
Flint	12
Lithium carbonate	8
Opax	10

White Crackle

Frit 3195	75
Feldspar	25

Rick's White Crackle

Potash feldspar	33.5
Frit W-15	41.5
Barium carbonate	14
Flint	11

Fat White (from Ken Vavrek)

Frit 3191	65
Ball clay	20
Colemanite	10
Alumina hydrate	5
Zircopax	20

White (from Howard Yana-Shapiro)

Gerstley borate	99
Potash feldspar	20
Flint	19
Ball clay	10
Barium carbonate	10

White

Gerstley borate	90
Ball clay	10
Zircopax	10

White

Gerstley borate	80
Buckingham feldspar	20
Opax	10

Matt White Crackle

Frit 3195	65
Feldspar	20
Kaolin	5
Whiting	10

White

Frit 3110	30
Gerstley borate	50
Nepheline syenite	20
Bentonite	2

White

Frit 3195	90
Feldspar	10
Ball clay	5

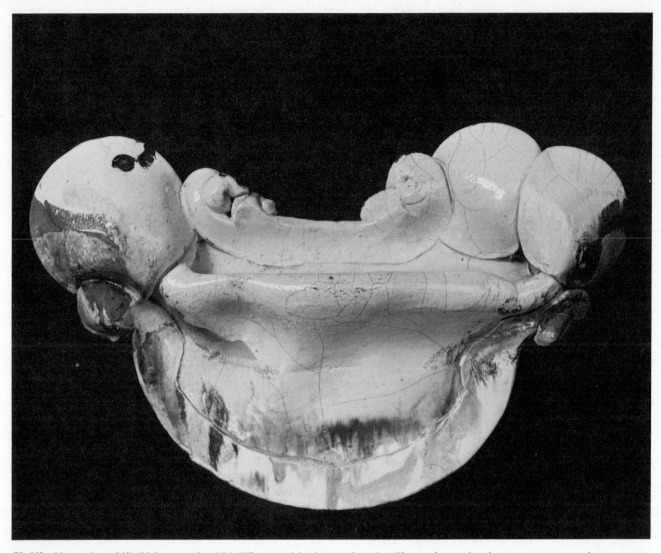

Shelf by Nancy Jurs. 20'' (50.8 cm) wide. 1974. White crackle glaze and oxides. The oxides on the glaze give a misty quality to a very solid form.

White

Colemanite (W-15)	60
Feldspar	40
Tin oxide	10

Copper Blue to Red (from Adele Zimmerman)

Frit 3134	45
Colemanite	40
Flint	7
Kaolin (EPK)	8

Add to base:

Copper carbonate	6%

Note: Good copper luster if piece is rapidly reduced and quickly cooled.

Red Raku (from Ken Vavrek)

Nepheline syenite	30
Frit 3230	20
Flint	20
Frit 3191	25
Whiting	5

Add to base:

Tin oxide	5%
Copper carbonate	3%
Red iron oxide	0.5%
Bentonite	1%

Note: To produce a good red, this glaze needs to be reduced in the kiln first and then reduced again in post-firing.

Tomats Red (from Carol Townsend)

Gerstley borate	50
Borax	50

Add to base:

Copper oxide	20%
Red iron oxide	5%

For blues, add to base:

Copper oxide	3%
Cobalt oxide	3%

Chartreuse Green (from Carol Townsend)

Gerstley borate	120
Frit 25	80
Tin oxide	4

Add to base:

Red iron oxide	1
Potassium bichromate	8

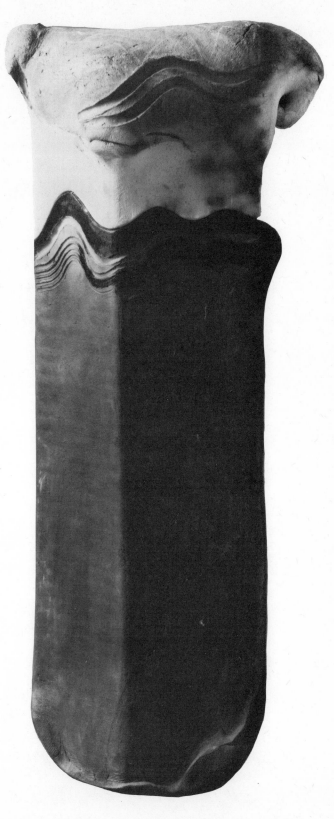

Raku Box *by Richard Hirsch. 12″ (30.5 cm) high. 1972. Slab construction, unglazed, smoked, black flocking.*

Seated Lady by Susan and Steven Kemenyffy.
32″ (81.3 cm) high. 1972.
Raku covered jar. Luster and fumed decoration.

Pale Lady by Susan and Steven Kemenyffy.
Approximately 48″ (121.9 cm) high.
Raku covered jar. Luster and fumed decoration.

Yellow *(from Adele Zimmerman)*

Frit 3134	80
Borax	10
Kaolin (EPK)	10

Add to base:

Vanadium stain	6%

Yellow

Frit P-25	36
Frit 3124	28
Kaolin	8
Flint	12

Add to base:

Lithium carbonate	8
Potassium bichromate	1%

Soda Blue

Frit 3110	70
Colemanite	50
Flint	10
Soda ash	10
Kaolin (EPK)	5

Purple *(from Adele Zimmerman)*

Frit 3134	40
Colemanite	40
Borax	10
Flint	10

Add to base:

Manganese dioxide	2%
Cobalt oxide	½%

Pink to Lavender *(from Adele Zimmerman)*

Frit 3134	70
Flint	5
Borax	10
Colemanite	10
Kaolin (EPK)	5

Add to base:

Hommel orchid glaze stain	6%

Iridescent Gold Luster

Soda ash	44.2
Frit W-15	30.9
Borax	18.6
Kaolin	24
Flint	65

For gold luster, add to base:

Silver nitrate	1%
Bismuth subnitrate	1%

For copper luster, add to base:

Red copper oxide	2%
Bismuth subnitrate	2%

Gold Luster *(from Adele Zimmerman)*

Colemanite	40
Borax	50
Flint	10
Silver nitrate	0.2

Gold Luster *(from Kit Yin-Ting Snyder)*

Colemanite	50
Borax	50
Silver nitrate	2.5

Black *(from Dave Lawson)*

Frit W-15	40
Barium carbonate	15
Nepheline syenite	15

Add to base:

Soda ash	1%
Black iron oxide	15%

Metallic Lusters

Metallic lusters have become one of the most characteristic elements in modern raku. One reason for this is that they produce magnificent colors with remarkable range. Also, luster effects are easily attained in raku, because of the smoking or reducing procedure built into the post-firing stage. The same formula may never duplicate exactly the same lustrous effects; lusters tend, therefore, to be useful in raku's reliance on change and unpredictability. In raku, metallic lusters offer a bright, shiny, colorful foil to the smoked, matte textures and blackened clay.

Essentially, metallic lusters are produced in raku by reducing certain metal oxides to their metallic form during the smoking period. Lead base glazes are the least successful because of the negative effect on them caused by harsh reduction. In reduction, lead may become a muddy, gunmetal color, which weakens the clarity of the luster. Metal oxides are usually added directly to the base glaze in the form of metal salts. In this form, the metal is totally dispersed throughout the glaze, and, because of its solubility, the metal migrates towards the surface where reduction takes place.

After the post-firing reducing period, a thin metallic

Theda Bara *by Marc Sijan. 18″ x 14″ (45.7 x 35.6 cm). Raku, luster, photographic decal, white crackle. Combining photographic technology with ceramic technology, this and the wall image on the opposite page retain a high degree of control.*

Electrical Workers by Marc Sijan. 19" x 14" (48.3 x 35.6 cm). Raku, luster, photographic decal.

film is left on the surface of the glaze. Partial in-kiln reduction during the firing cycle helps develop the film, so the metallic oxide will be slightly reduced even before the smoking takes place. Usually, the hotter the glaze comes out of the kiln, and the sooner it is in place in the reducing atmosphere, the stronger the luster effects will be. Care should be taken not to remove the pot from the post-firing reducing atmosphere too soon, as it may still be hot enough to reoxidize.

This overall luster should not be confused with luster solutions which are put on an already melted glaze. Usually, the latter is used as a form of overglaze decoration and is either sprayed or painted on a clean, smooth, melted glaze surface. Luster solutions of this type are composed of the metal salt, a natural resin, and an oily medium such as oil of lavender. After the solution is put on the ware, it is fired to red heat, and the resin burns, producing carbon which reduces the metal salt. A thin metal film is thus deposited as an overglaze layer. Lusters of this kind were perfected by the Persians around the 12th and 13th centuries.

Although this is not the usual way to develop lusters in raku, overglaze lusters can be made from various chemical solutions. Chemicals such as silver nitrate, bismuth subnitrate, tin chloride, gold chloride, and ferric chloride can be added directly to the base glaze. Each produces certain distinct colors; for example, silver will produce shades of yellow, and bismuth yields mother-of-pearl iridescence.

Lusters can be delicate and subtle, yet sometimes they become gaudy, reminding one of cheap, commercial, souvenir ceramics. Potters in raku who use them are ultimately responsible for their outcome.

Commercial Glazes

Commercially prepared glazes can be, and are, used in raku. Like those based on lead, boron, or the alkalies, the ones used for raku are usually in the low temperature range. Commercial glazes come in either dry powder form or as a liquid mixture. Many raku potters use them because they offer a very wide range of unique colors, colors which are often difficult or impossible to obtain with just straight additions of the coloring oxides into the low temperature bases. Commercial glazes are very predictable and they usually melt easily into a smooth surface. The color is always consistent. Most commercial glazes have a wide temperature range, thus ensuring good glaze melt and a range of effects. Because most commercially prepared glazes come mixed with some form of gum, they are easily applied to bisque ware and they are especially easy to brush on.

Some drawbacks to these glazes are that they suffer from being too predictable, show little effect from post-firing, are not easily reduced, and sometimes appear to look like applied paint.

Most commercially sold glazes are fairly expensive and therefore not practical, especially if large quantities are needed.

Coloring Oxide Solutions

One other possibility should be mentioned for use in raku glazing. The metallic coloring oxides can be applied over raku glazes, as a form of overglaze decoration. Usually metallic oxides in the form of soluble salts work best, because they dissolve and mix easily in water. Sometimes the coloring salts are combined with a low temperature frit to ensure a complete, smooth melt. These solutions work somewhat like a ceramic form of watercolor. Thin layers of these solutions are brushed on the dry surface of the glaze. When fired, these thin coatings can yield clear, beautiful colors, can be overlapped and sometimes can be iridescent or lustered, depending on their composition. Following is a group of oxide compositions given in parts by weight. These compositions should be thinned with water. Combinations can be used to produce different results.

Green

Potassium bichromate	10
Frit 3110	5

Turquoise or Lusters

Copper sulfate or Cupric chloride	10
Frit 3110	5

Blues

Cobalt chloride	10
Frit 3110	5

Brownish Purple

Manganese dioxide	10
Frit 3110	5

Green

Nickel chloride	10
Frit 3110	5

Gold Iridescence

Bismuth subnitrate	10
Silver nitrate	5
Frit 3110	5

Raku Engobes

Engobes can offer an alternative to, or work in conjunction with, raku glazes. Essentially, engobes are clay coatings or colored slips. They are usually applied to wet or

Bottle *by Paul Soldner. 19" (48.3 cm) high. 1968. Raku. Pots from this period of Soldner's work show a unique quality of glaze and clay handling. The positive/negative patch pattern of the surface is unified with a parallel treatment of the clay in the foot and neck.*

Boxes by Bill Stewart.
9″ (22.9 cm) high. 1971.
Slab and cast parts, commercial glazes.

damp clay because they must closely match the shrinkage rate of the clay body. Usually the formulas for engobes closely match that of the actual clay body being used. When applied and fired correctly they vitrify into a hard, dense layer that fits the clay body without checking or peeling off. Engobes can be used by themselves but most often are put underneath transparent or semiopaque glazes. In this case the engobe coating should not dissolve or bleed into the covering glaze.

Most engobe formulas are made up primarily of clay. Clays that fire to a pale color, such as kaolin or ball clay, are used to produce clean and clear colors in the engobe. Most engobes for high fire stoneware require a large proportion of clay in their formulas. However, since raku is most often fired in the low temperature range, raku engobes are formulated with a minimum amount of refractory clay. A slip or clay coating of this type that has a minimum of clay, and therefore considerably less shrinkage, and also fires to a hard, dense, opaque layer, is called a vitreous engobe.

The compositions of vitreous engobes used in raku are very similar to glaze formulas used in the low temperature range. Possibly the only differences are that more clay and usually more flint are required in the vitreous engobes than in the glazes. A low temperature frit and fluxes like borax or talc added to both the clay and flint complete the normal vitreous engobe composition. Colorants are then added to the base formula as in glazes.

Vitreous engobes have the advantage that because of their low shrinkage rate they can be applied to dry clay or bisque ware. Because of their clay content, it is extremely easy to brush them on the ware, and once fired they offer chromatic and textural possibilities that are different from raku glazes. Following are two engobe bases given in parts by weight.

Vitreous Base

Tennessee #5 ball clay	20
Flint	30
Frit 3191	25
Talc	10
Borax	5

For white, add to base:

| Opax | 10 |

For reddish copper luster, add to base:

| Red iron oxide | 5 |
| Red copper oxide | 5 |

Base (from Ken Vavrek)

Ball clay	20
Flint	30
Frit 14	25
Talc	10

Conclusion

Few people have the desire to study clay and glaze theory for its own sake. At the same time, obviously, advance knowledge can be an invaluable tool for the potter who may one day need a certain effect for an idea he has had and can draw on his theoretical knowledge to help him achieve it. Many potters manage to find their balancing point between knowing too much theory and too little. Ideally, the technical information and the idea of the pot will mesh, so that the pot is not a compromise but is a complete expression of a process and an idea, and of a mind which comprehends them both.

Bottle by Paul Soldner.
27" x 6" (68.6 x 15.2 cm).
Wheel thrown, iron and copper brush design,
smoked after firing at cone 010–08.
This is distinctive of Soldner's
recent work and shows a typical
understanding of balance.

Bottle by Paul Soldner (front and back views). 16″ (40.6 cm) high. Wheel thrown, iron and copper decoration on copper engobe, clear glaze coating, salt vapor firing. Though less monochromatic than his early raku pots, these later pots also achieve a richness and retain the subtlety which Soldner sought originally from the medium. This pot also reveals the dual influences of abstract expressionism and Japanese brushwork.

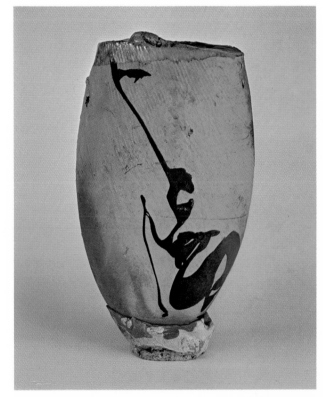

Vase by Paul Soldner (front and back views). 14″ (35.6 cm) high. Wheel thrown, foot added, iron copper brush design on copper engobe, salt fired for vapor effect. Soldner is again expanding the raku process to include salt vapor.

Platter by Jun Kaneko. 12 1/2" x 12 1/2" (31.8 x 31.8 cm). 1971. In its rough, simple form and vigorous color, this platter possibly has its roots in the raku style of Kenzan I.

Gold Shell Plate *by Richard Hirsch. 20″ (50.8 cm) in diameter. 1971.*
Slab, impressed, silver nitrate, bismuth sub-nitrate added to the base glaze.
A juxtaposition of the soft, smoked slab and the shiny, metallic glaze,
provide an excitement of surface and form.

Raku Box *by Richard Hirsch. 4″ x 4″ x 6″ (10.2 x 10.2 x 15.2 cm).*
Slab impressed, clear glaze, fumed with iron chloride and tin chloride.
The functional aspect of this pot is secondary to the softness
of its slab construction and its other sculptural qualities.

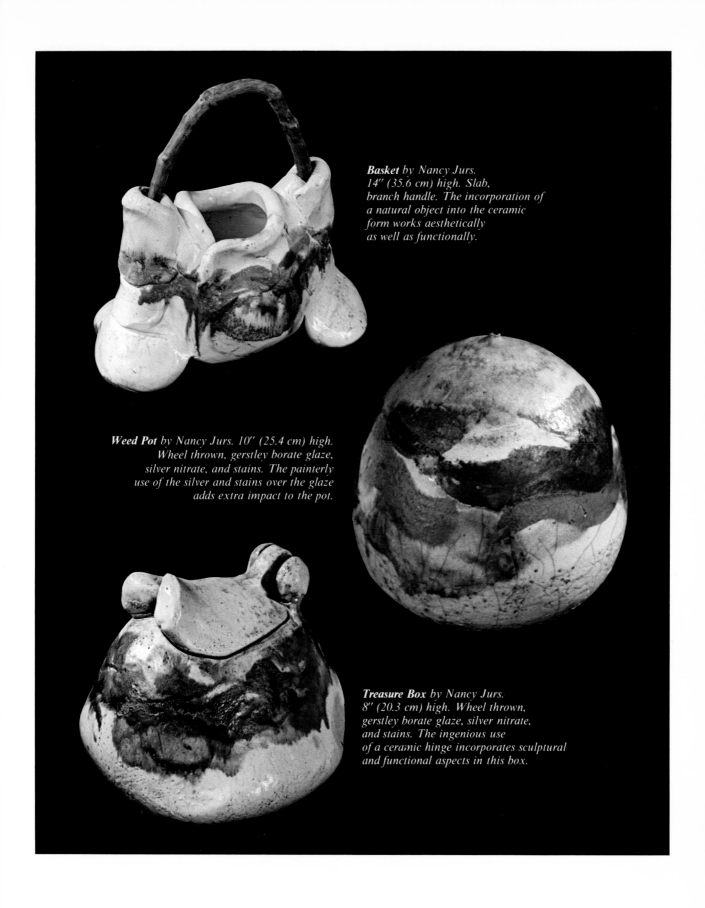

Basket by Nancy Jurs.
14″ (35.6 cm) high. Slab,
branch handle. The incorporation of
a natural object into the ceramic
form works aesthetically
as well as functionally.

Weed Pot by Nancy Jurs. 10″ (25.4 cm) high.
Wheel thrown, gerstley borate glaze,
silver nitrate, and stains. The painterly
use of the silver and stains over the glaze
adds extra impact to the pot.

Treasure Box by Nancy Jurs.
8″ (20.3 cm) high. Wheel thrown,
gerstley borate glaze, silver nitrate,
and stains. The ingenious use
of a ceramic hinge incorporates sculptural
and functional aspects in this box.

Covered Jar by Ken Ferguson (opposite page). 22″ (55.9 cm) high.
Ferguson has a reputation in stoneware, yet has adapted his forms in a way
wholly appropriate to raku. The form is powerful and quiet.

Orange Tea Bowl. *Iron chloride spray over a clear base glaze fired in an electric kiln and then smoked.*

Golden Tea Bowl. *Bismuth sub-nitrate and silver nitrate in a base glaze. This tea bowl, unlike Oriental tea bowls, was thrown on the potter's wheel. Both tea bowls by Richard Hirsch.*

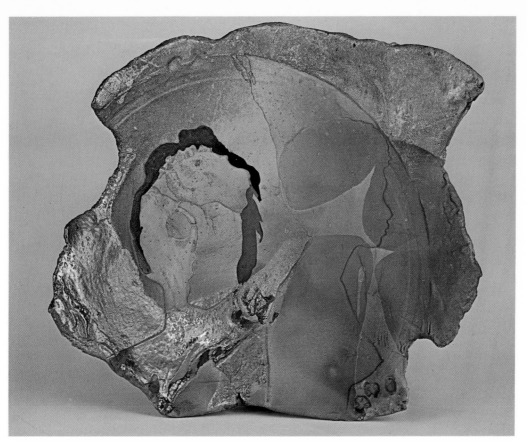

Beetle Pot *by Paul Soldner. 21″ x 20″ (53.3 x 50.8 cm). Engobes, embossed design, clear glaze, low fired.*

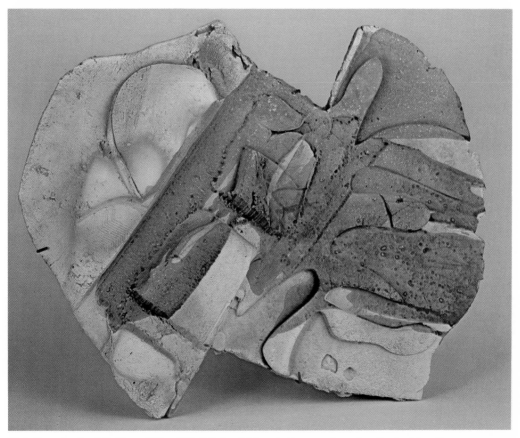

Slab Form *by Paul Soldner. 23″ x 20″ (58.4 x 50.8 cm). Copper glaze, low fired with salt vapor.*

Playboy Centerfold *by Paul Soldner. 24″ x 19″ (61 x 48.3 cm). Embossed design, copper glaze, clear glaze with engobes, light post-smoking.*

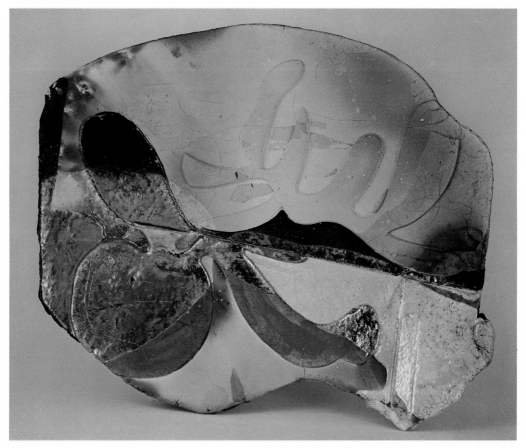

Form *by Paul Soldner. 23″ x 19″ (58.4 x 48.3 cm). Engobes, embossed design, copper glaze, salt vapor firing.*

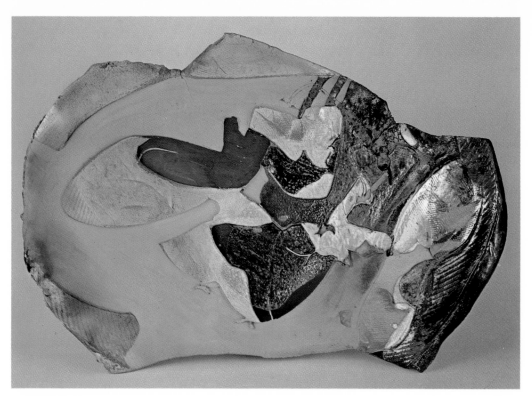

Slab Form by Paul Soldner. 21″ x 19″ (53.3 x 48.3 cm). Engobes, embossed design, clear glaze, low fired at cone 010–08 with salt vapor.

Slab Form by Paul Soldner. 23″ x 20″ (58.4 x 50.8 cm). Engobes, embossed design, copper glaze, low fired with salt vapor.

Strawberry Plate by Richard Hirsch. 22" (55.9 cm) diameter. 1970.
Slab. The most distinctive aspect of this plate is the use
of gold chloride added to the base glaze to achieve a unique color.
The relaxed and rough construction provides a foil to the soft,
elusive range of colors in the glaze.

Goblets by Marguerite Antell.
3″ to 6″ (7.6 to 15.2 cm) high.
Raku and kiln reduction.
A strong use of color and
a tendency to art nouveau
in the forms complement each
other in this group of goblets.

Pumpkin Form Vase by Richard Hirsch. Unglazed, smoked, iron chloride spray. 1974. The color introduced by the iron chloride spray under the smoked impressions relates to the vegetable form.

Squash Form Vase by Richard Hirsch. 23" x 26" (58.4 x 66 cm). 1974. Wheel thrown and coiled, unglazed with iron chloride spray, smoked. The organic references of this pot include the form and the use of selected grasses impressed on the pot as part of the post-firing process.

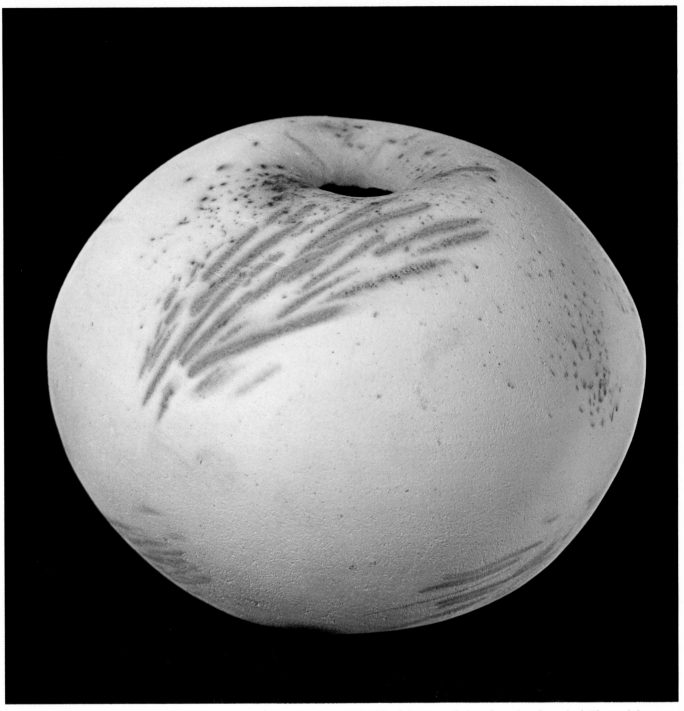

Apple Form Vase *by Richard Hirsch. 12″ x 15″ (30.5 x 38.1 cm). 1974. Wheel thrown and altered, unglazed, smoked. The seeds burst from the applied grasses and spattered against the heated pot, leaving their marks in the post-firing process.*

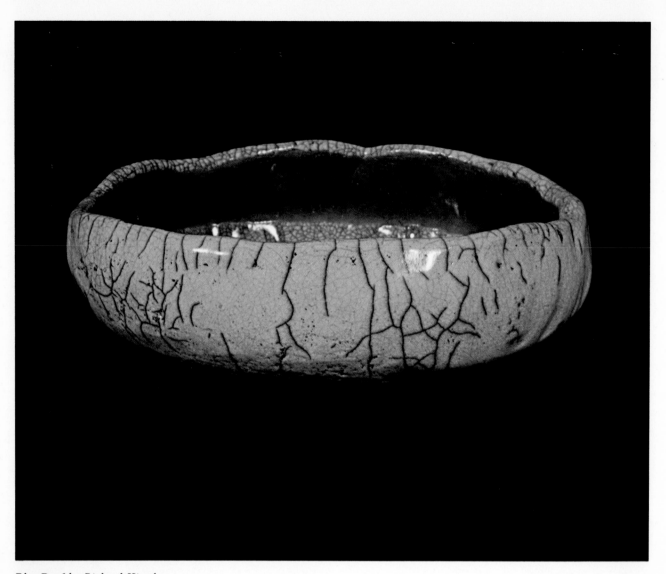

Rice Bowl *by Richard Hirsch.*
Partially glazed, smoked, pinched. 1974.
The forming method was used directly
to create the form; the Oriental
influence is undeniable.

5

Kilns: Requirements, Construction, and Use

Most raku pots are fired twice. The bisque firing is usually conducted in an entirely conventional manner in whatever kiln is available. The second firing of raku ware, however, usually involves a kiln which is somewhat different from those used in processes other than raku. This chapter deals specifically with kilns for the second raku firing, and tries to make clear the relationship between the particular options in raku firing and post-firing and the special requirements these options impose on the kiln used.

Requirements

The purpose of a kiln is to create and retain sufficient heat around a pot for the body to mature, or for the glaze to melt satisfactorily. The main requirement for any kiln is that the draft, or movement of air, in the kiln be such that heat is evenly distributed with a minimum of loss and a controlled increase. Certain kiln chamber shapes are more efficient in this respect than others: a cube-shaped kiln lends itself to more even heat distribution than a long, rectangular kiln.

Three factors govern the shape and construction of a kiln: the temperature required, the heat source, and whether or not the kiln is required to be permanent. Generally speaking, the higher the temperature required, the more sophisticated a kiln has to be. The choice of heat source can also determine the design of the kiln. The main sources are: wood, gas, oil, and electricity. A raku kiln tends to be temporary mainly because it is often advisable to rebuild it to accommodate a pot of large size or unusual shape.

A raku kiln should reach 1800°F. (982°C.) comfortably. This is earthenware temperature, and therefore the kiln need be of only moderate sophistication. It is not as simple as an open-pit fire, nor does it need to be as complicated as a high-fire stoneware or porcelain kiln.

The fact that the raku potter will probably want to remove his pots from the kiln when they are still red-hot creates the single most important requirement in the raku kiln, a factor not present in kilns designed for most other processes. In order to ensure that the pots can be removed quickly and safely, the kiln must be designed with easy access as a priority.

Despite the complication of this important requirement, most kilns made for raku are relatively simple, fairly cheap, and easy for the potter to construct.

The design of your kiln and its site will be determined to some extent by the source of energy you use. It may also happen in reverse: that the source of energy you use will be determined by the factors of design and available site. All of these questions should be taken into consideration before you finally make a decision about the details of your kiln.

Wood-Burning Kilns

The traditional Japanese raku kiln was fired by wood. (The temporary raku kiln traditionally used charcoal as a fuel.) The need for a firebox attached to the kiln chamber substantially determines the design of the kiln as a whole. The convenience and expense of wood as a fuel will mainly depend on whether your site is rural or is at least within reach of adequate wood supplies. Provided that the problem of supply is not severe, wood firing is a most worthwhile experience.

Wood as a Fuel. Softwoods (i.e., pine, spruce, fir, cedar, etc.), although they burn at a lower temperature, are preferable to hardwoods (maple, beech, oak, etc.), be-

Joan Campbell of Australia firing her kiln made of brick cut to form a circular shape. The bricks are held together with a welded frame. She reduces much of her raku in a pit.

cause they release heat faster. The wood should be cut into lengths 1″ or 2″ (2.5 or 5.1 cm) shorter than the firebox, and split into thin pieces of various sizes, down to 1″ x 2″. The pieces of wood can be bigger during the early stages of the firing, when you want a cautious heat increase. Off-cuts from a sawmill provide a good source of fuel, as do scraps from construction sites. The cost of the wood will obviously vary according to your environment and the availability of the fuel.

Beginning from a cold kiln, the first firing will take about 2 to 3 hours to reach temperature. The second firing will take about 45 minutes. After this, the firings even out to about 30 minutes, depending on how little heat is lost when the kiln is opened to complete the previous firing, and depending also on the size of the pots. Larger pots take longer, and should be heated up more slowly.

Firing with wood is very direct. For example, to get the final few degrees of heat which melts the glaze, and to hold it there, may take some energetic stoking! You learn much, even if you are experienced in kiln firing, about combustion, draft, oxidation and reduction, and much about kilns in general while firing a raku wood kiln.

Bear in mind that wood firing takes time and work. Not only must the wood be cut and split, but also it should be stacked and stored where it can remain dry, yet where the air can get at it. The fire will need constant tending. There is a great expenditure of time and energy in preparing and using the fuel for relatively few pots.

At the temperatures required for raku, wood as a fuel does not seem to have any special chemical or physical effect on the resulting pot. If a potter places great importance on the finished piece, he may not wish to fire with wood. On the other hand, it may increase the importance of a certain pot for the potter to know that it was fired in a time-honored way, and in a traditional raku kiln. It is easy to see how some potters (notably Hal Riegger) feel that wood firing is particularly in accord with the nature of raku.

Kiln Design. Design your kiln with more than adequate draft capacity. The plan should include a grate that allows ash to drop into a pit underneath, so that the grate itself will support mainly burning wood. The ash pit should have approximately twice the volume of the firebox. We recommend that the grate should slant diagonally down toward the kiln chamber. This warms all the air entering the kiln chamber and allows the possibility of a fast firing.

In the firing chamber, you may use either a sagger, or a kiln shelf as a floor, to avoid direct flame on the pot. Usually a space of 1½″ to 2″ (3.8 to 5.1 cm) is left between the kiln wall and the sagger or kiln shelf.

The pots are removed from a traditional Japanese raku kiln through the top of the kiln chamber. Therefore, the flue must be easily moveable when hot, so that you can look down into the kiln, both to check on the glaze melt, and to remove the pots when they are ready. The

flue should be adjustable too, so that you can use it to control the draft.

If you build the modified, corbeled arch wood-burning kiln (see pages 120–123), the door will be on the opposite side of the kiln chamber from the firebox. The door should be light enough to be picked up without effort.

Should you want a reduction atmosphere in the kiln, one thing you will need is a door that fits tight to the firebox.

Kiln Site. Check the local bylaws for fire regulations. It might be illegal to have a wood-burning kiln in the neighborhood you select for your kiln site.

A wood fire offers its own particular hazards, and flying sparks can be made more dangerous by a strong wind or by the proximity of long grass, wood buildings, or gasoline tanks.

Some potters prefer to build their wood-burning kilns partly into a hillside. This necessitates some digging, but the bank supports the kiln, helps eliminate side drafts, and insulates the kiln. The bank also provides the potter a place to stand above the kiln chamber to bring the ware out through the flue.

If there is a prevailing wind, use it as a draft, building your kiln so that the breeze will naturally enter the firebox, and travel into the kiln chamber and out at the flue.

Organize your area for wood storage so that you do not have far to carry the wood, yet in such a place that it does not present a fire hazard, should sparks fly. If you are splitting wood while you are firing, you will need an area for this so that people are out of the way of your axe! Keep your axe *blunt*, wear strong-toed boots, and split the wood lengthwise.

Using the Kiln. There is much more control with wood as a fuel than might be expected. You may wish to choose literally each piece of wood with regard to its size or type as you stoke at critical moments. The heat will not increase too fast at the beginning of the firing, but you can use larger pieces of wood to ensure that no sudden heat will crack the pots. The main problem you will encounter is keeping an even increase of heat in the kiln. The pots will break unless the heat rises at a steady rate in the early stages of firing. Don't let the fire burn too low, and stoke it regularly, but not too fast or the fire could become choked with unburnt wood.

Keep your eye on the chimney. If steam (white in color) issues from it, your wood is wet and heat is being wasted. If smoke (gray or black in color) issues from it, then carbon particles are coming out, and combustion is incomplete, creating a premature reduction. This means that there is too much wood for the amount of oxygen. Probably the draft is inadequate, so you should stoke slower, or there are obstructions in the way of the air entering the firebox that should be removed. There should be no heavy black smoke coming from the chimney in the early stages, though you will almost certainly get flames out the top as the firing continues. However, if you want a semi-reduction atmosphere, add more wood than the oxygen can burn.

Toward the end of the firing you will probably need to achieve and maintain all the heat you can coax from the fire. Stoke small pieces—they should virtually explode in the firebox. To provide more heat, you may also rake the embers flat in the ash pit and build an additional fire there. This will give you more heat for a short while, though after a time it can choke the draft under the fire.

Note: For those aspects of firing that apply generally to all kilns, see Chapter 7 on *Firing and Post-Firing*.

Conclusions. The kind of experience offered by wood firing can only be described by such hackneyed words as "thrilling" or "rewarding." The experience itself, however, is not hackneyed; wood is probably the fuel with the closest rapport to the material and the process, and is an enjoyable, romantic way of firing. You will probably become totally occupied by the kiln and the pots in it, and gain proficiency and experience in the intimate aspects of firing.

Gas Kilns

Gas is introduced into kilns through burner ports. Burners are an integral part of the kiln (see section on *Burners* later in this chapter). Because gas burns very hot, tremendously high temperatures can be reached in a short time.

Gas as a Fuel. It is better with gas to be conservative in firing and to heat the pots slowly, especially if they are large. While the need for caution with explosive fuels must be emphasized, gas remains a fairly safe source of energy. It is widely available and is extremely practical, quick to heat up the kiln, and clean to use.

Both natural gas and propane gas can be used for raku. Propane gas is a petroleum by-product and is contained under pressure. In the tank, it is part liquid and part vapor. Because it is under such pressure, atmospheric burners using primary and secondary air are quite sufficient. As propane issues out of the burner orifice, it vaporizes and ignites easily. Propane gas is portable and comes in canisters of 25 lbs., 50 lbs., 100 lbs., 500 lbs. (11.3 kg. to 226.5 kg.), and even larger. The 100 lb. (45.3 kg.) size is often used for a temporary kiln and the largest size can be used for a permanent one.

When firing with propane, make sure you have enough to last for the entire firing. The process of disconnecting and reconnecting canisters can interrupt the firing, thereby losing heat in the kiln, and the resulting heat fluctuation can break the pots. Either buy a big enough canister or manifold (connect) together two smaller canisters. (When purchasing the canisters from the gas company, you can get the piping and instructions for manifolding.)

To obtain maximum pressure when a smaller tank is nearly empty, lay it down on its side. Watch the regulator and avoid taking too much gas out at once, otherwise the tank ices up and you lose pressure.

Take all precautions to avoid leakage of the gas. When connecting the gas line to the canisters, always make sure that the valves are securely closed. Propane is heavier than air and can collect for quite a while without being noticed. For this reason do not put the kiln or canisters close to a basement. Check all connections by sniffing them; the smell of propane gas is unmistakable. The high-pressure hoses should be long enough to keep the canisters of gas at least 10' to 15' (3 to 4.6 m) away from the kiln itself. Do not leave the kiln unattended because wind can blow out the burners in the early stages of firing.

Natural gas is piped through city mains and gives very little problem for a permanent kiln, though it is impractical for a portable one. Sometimes there may be too little mains pressure for firing, and forced air burners (see section on Burners later in this chapter) are sometimes needed. Natural gas is already in vapor form and ignites easily. Once you have a meter, and the connections are made, you never have to worry about interrupted firings and in the long run it is cheaper than propane.

The leakage of natural gas is not much of a problem ordinarily, because the permanent piping usually requires professional installation. The major precaution necessary is to be sure that both the main valve and the valves at the burners are turned off properly after the day's firing. The smell of mains natural gas is easily detected.

Kiln Design. For a gas kiln, a cube shape is ideal for efficient draft and even heat distribution. To help with heat distribution, target bricks are often placed inside the kiln directly in front of the burners. These bricks split the flame and direct heat to all parts of the kiln. Above the target bricks is a false kiln floor made with a kiln shelf, supported by bricks placed on their side, elevating the false floor 4" (10.2 cm) above the *real* floor. The shelf protects the pots from direct flame and, as with most kilns that protect pots in this way, a gap of 1½" to 2" (3.8 to 5.1 cm) is left between the false floor and the kiln walls to allow an efficient draft. Burner ports must be included in the kiln walls. The ports should be large enough to bring secondary air into the kiln if you are using atmospheric burners, in which case a port of 4½" x 2" (11.4 x 5.1 cm) is sufficient—it certainly should not be larger than 4½" x 4½" (11.4 x 11.4 cm). Generally a port the size of a half-brick is sufficient. For further information, see Burners.

Kiln Site. If the kiln is to be located indoors, you must provide an efficient exhaust system because burnt gas gives off toxic fumes. It is dangerous to have a kiln indoors and unvented. Temporary kilns are best situated outside where, naturally, no venting is necessary.

A kiln made from hard firebrick, designed and built by Norman and Ann Mortimer. A welded frame door fits on the side and two propane burners are positioned to create a crossdraft. The flue is covered with a metal cylinder which acts as a chimney. The chimney is anchored by wire to the kiln.

Betty Woodman shows the swing door of her brick catenary arch raku kiln.

Using the Kiln. Gas is such a hot fuel that care must be taken not to heat up the kiln too fast, as this can destroy the ware. A high-pressure regulator is an important item in controlling the heat, as it directly regulates the amount of gas going through the burners into the kiln.

The time taken to fire is difficult to estimate, except by experience, because it depends not only on the size of the kiln but on the size of the ware in the kiln, the amount of ware in the kiln, and, to a certain extent, on the climate. We can take as an example, however, the typical situation of a small—18″ x 18″ x 18″ (45.7 x 45.7 x 45.7 cm) inside dimension—cold kiln, containing six tea bowls. In this situation, it will take at least 1 hour to complete the firing. Subsequent firings, after the kiln has been warmed up, will take about half as long.

In the following example, where reference is made to the gas pressure, it must be borne in mind that the pressure is controlled by the tank regulator. The amount of gas passing through the burners is determined by the orifice size of the burner. With an increase in orifice size, a correspondingly lower pressure reading is required on the regulator. The figures below refer to the author's burners discussed later in this chapter.

When firing, turn on the gas initially with barely enough pressure to keep the burners lit. Turn up the kiln by ½ lb. p.s.i. (per square inch) at intervals of about 10 to 15 minutes until the glazes start to melt. Too much gas pressure will change the atmosphere in the kiln, and the presence of unburnt gas could blister the glazes. About 5 lbs. pressure is a sufficient maximum.

If the pots are large, heat up the kiln proportionately more slowly. A firing may take 2 or 3 hours, or even longer. Some potters prefer to use a lot of gas pressure because it shortens the firing time, but we do not necessarily recommend this because of the possibility of loss through blistering and cracking.

Conclusion. Gas is in many respects the ideal fuel for raku kilns, even though it has the serious disadvantage of being extremely explosive. Gas, however, is convenient and easy to control. When you use the proper equipment, such as high-pressure hoses, a regulator, and brass fittings, there is little physical difficulty involved in the firing process in comparison to a wood kiln (see Burners). Gas *is* a dangerous fuel, but with common sense and constant watching for telltale signs of problems, it is the fuel most likely to satisfy the majority of demands for the raku potter.

Oil Kilns

Oil kilns are substantially the same as gas kilns in design, but the burner system and the construction material required may need to be more sophisticated. Oil kilns are popular, despite the complicated equipment they require.

Oil as a Fuel. Because oil is a liquid and is not stored under pressure, more heat is concentrated in a given quantity than with natural gas, propane, or wood. In theory it is also safer than gas, because it does not burn easily until evaporated into an explosive gas.

Being a liquid, oil needs to combine with more air for combustion, and, for this reason, air pressure is more important for oil than for gas. The combustion of oil is incomplete below 1000°F. (538°C.), as it must be in vapor form in order to burn completely, and difficulty is to be expected in the early stages of firing. Some potters recommend that the early stages be fired with gas or kerosene, and then, when the kiln has heated sufficiently to vaporize the oil, a change be made to oil, as it is more efficient in the later stages of firing.

A good grade firebrick is needed for a kiln to be fired with oil, because the heat from the burners and the chemicals in the fuel may melt or erode the brick. Soft insulation brick is particularly inadvisable for oil fired kilns.

Secondary air is not needed with the forced air burners usually required for oil, and in fact, should be excluded as it cools the firebox. Therefore, the burner nozzles should be sealed against the burner ports to ensure exclusion of cool air.

With oil as a fuel, the firing is easy to control and the fuel reserve is easy to measure. The kiln atmosphere can be regulated and a rapid heat increase is possible.

Among the disadvantages of oil are the uncertainty of supply and price, and the fact that oil is the dirtiest fuel considered here, being smoky and smelly.

Kiln Design. The usual feed of the oil from the tank to the burners is by gravity, so that the tank must be higher than the burners. The burners can be fed by drip, or pumps can be incorporated into the system. You will need at least 15′ (4.6m) of pipe between the tank and the kiln for safety's sake to keep the oil reservoir from the heat source.

The design of the kiln chamber for an oil fired kiln will be similar to that for a gas kiln.

Using the Kiln. Preheat the firebox to help evaporation of the liquid oil. Unburnt oil will not disperse as gas does, but will accumulate, unless the kiln is attended and adjusted constantly during firing. An accumulation of unburnt oil can occur, and with it the danger of explosion.

Conclusions. The certainty of supply and price will probably be a big factor in choosing oil as your fuel. The versatility and complexity of the burner system must be considered also, before a decision can be reached.

Electric Kilns

A kiln heated by electricity works simply by putting an electric current through a resistant wire usually wound in

Wood Burning Kiln

This traditional Japanese wood-burning kiln can be built into a bank to support the structure, cut down side drafts, and enable the potter easier access to the kiln chamber to remove the ware. The kiln pictured below was built by the authors in the open to show the structure better.

1. *A cement block pad is laid and leveled. Then the firebox is constructed based on the size of the kiln shelves available and the width of the pots to be fired. The firebox is also leveled.*

2. *Metal rods are used to make the grate that the wood will rest on. The area below will become the ash pit during firing.*

3. *The metal rods are spaced between the bricks. The open areas are filled with clay. In this kiln the rods used were too thin and buckled from the intense heat.*

4. *The door of the firebox has an opening at the bottom to draw in air so that the wood has sufficient oxygen to burn.*

5. *The ware chamber is polygonal and also acts as the chimney. The spaces between the bricks later are also filled up with clay.*

Corbeled Arch Kiln

This is an updraft, corbeled arch kiln with the flue at the top. It uses K23 or K26 soft insulation brick in its construction.

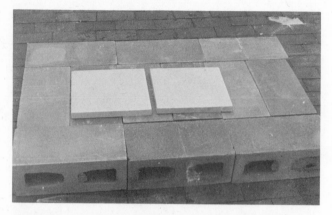

1. Two kiln shelves are placed on a leveled cement block pad to give the approximate size of the kiln chamber required.

2. Target bricks placed in front of the burner ports inside the kiln break up the flame and distribute the heat from the burners. Target bricks are necessary in this case because the burners are both on the same side of the kiln (see 6 on opposite page), and the heat might not be evenly distributed otherwise.

3. The kiln walls are built up about 1 1/2" (3.8 cm) away from the kiln shelf to ensure correct draft. The shelf is resting on soft firebricks turned on their sides.

4. The roof of the kiln is built by the corbeled arch method. This is simply a stepping-in process. Each time a brick is laid, it is hung inside a bit more than the previous one until a step-like arch is made. The heavier red housebricks are used as a counterbalance.

5. *Front view.*

6. *Back view.*

coils. These coils are made out of nichrome or Kanthal, and are high temperature elements. These elements are wired throughout the kiln, thus ensuring an even distribution of heat. An even heat produces an even glaze melt. Electricity is the source least used for raku, because the process of constant heating and cooling is hard on the elements, bricks, switches, and casing.

Advantages and Disadvantages. An electric kiln will give even heat distribution; also you have good control over the heat increase through the switch mechanisms, and there is no difficulty reaching raku temperatures. Electricity is a clean fuel, and if you already have an electric kiln, you may wish to use it to investigate the possibilities of raku before investing in a kiln more practical for this process.

Besides the major disadvantage of wear to the kiln, there are other practical difficulties with electric kilns. Most of them are commercially produced in a very complete form, and come in a wide range of qualities, shapes, and sizes. If you don't have one already, the expense is probably prohibitive if you intend to use it primarily for a raku glaze firing. To construct your own electric kiln is possible, but you should have the tools and the technical knowledge to groove the bricks for the elements, to deal with the problems of wiring, and so on. Special 220 volt wiring is necessary for the kiln, and you should always get qualified advice and inspection to meet safety standards. Electric kilns are not usually portable, if only because they must be used near to a 220 outlet, and, though some models can be adapted by height, you cannot make them wider, so that the size of your pots may be restricted by the kiln.

Even if all these other problems did not exist, an electric kiln is not ideal for the process of a raku firing. Reduction is only possible in the kiln if you introduce a combustible substance into it, which is difficult, time consuming, and damaging to the elements. The spyhole in electric kilns is generally too small, and is placed so as to prevent the potter from seeing any pot completely, let alone those at the other end of the kiln. The only way of seeing the pots properly is to open the door, which is dangerous, loses heat, and also can damage the kiln. The loss of contact with the pot during the firing caused by the inherent structure of the kiln is a serious technical disadvantage and quite simply goes against the nature of the raku process. It can also prove expensive, for if the pots are overfired, the glaze can run and, besides ruining shelves and furniture (a possibility with overfiring in any kiln), can stick to and irreparably damage the electrical elements.

Safety. If you do use an electric kiln, you should take care that the metal tongs do not touch the elements, as in some cases a severe shock can result. Less drastic but also important is the danger from the heat in the kiln when it is first opened. This is, of course, true of firing in any raku kiln, but especially so with electric kilns which are often supported on stands and are therefore directly at face level. Because it is located indoors, there may be unpleasant fumes and certainly a great deal of heat from an electric kiln, so that an efficient ventilation system is a decided advantage. The post-firing may have to be indoors also, with the attendant discomfort of confined smoke if the room is unventilated.

Using the Kiln. Because of the automatic control allowed by the switch mechanisms, electric kilns are probably one of the easiest kinds to use. Most kilns have two or more elements and some have separate switches for each element. With this type, the gradual heat increase is obtained by switching on first one, then two, then three elements. Other types have one switch which, by means of a rheostat, increases the resistance of the elements. These switches vary too, but commonly they have three settings: low, medium, and high.

The rate of heat increase in an electric kiln is relatively slow and there is little danger of firing too fast. After the first firing, the elements and bricks are hot and the firing schedule will be faster, but the potter is still dependent on the speed of the elements themselves.

Conclusions. If the only kiln available to you is heated by electricity, you should certainly use it. However, if you intend to work in raku to any large extent, we do not recommend that you buy an electric kiln, not only because the initial expense of buying one is much higher than necessary for a raku glaze firing, and the process is unduly hard on the equipment, but also because the nature of this kiln does not lend itself to the immediacy between the potter, the pot, and the kiln which is so much a part of raku. There is little opportunity for control of atmosphere, which can limit the range of accidental effects obtainable on the pot. In addition, the size and shape of the kiln may limit the size and shape of your pots, and the slow heat increase means that not many firings can be completed in a given day.

Construction Materials

Kilns require materials that will stand up consistently to high temperatures. The main construction material is brick, but we shall also deal here with alternative materials which are practical for certain purposes.

Bricks. Bricks are made of fired clay and are chosen for kilns with their refractory properties in mind; that is, their ability to withstand high temperature. Of course, bricks are not indestructible and are liable to deteriorate through cracking or spalling (when flakes of material fall off the brick, weakening and eventually destroying it).

The factors which determine your choice of brick for raku are, besides cost, the maximum temperature to be reached, the life span of the brick, and its reaction to continual heating and cooling. For example, some brick, such as hard firebrick, takes a long while to heat up, but also retains its heat for some time. A kiln made of this kind of brick will not cool down much in the course of a day's firing, which may increase the number of possible firings. However, a pot introduced into a hot kiln may explode, especially if it is a large closed form. A knowledge of the behavior of the brick you can select will obviously help you.

The basic choices of brick for raku are: common red or buff brick, hard firebrick, and soft firebrick or insulation brick.

Common Red or Common Buff Brick. Common red bricks or house bricks can be used for raku, though there are two factors limiting their use: Red brick melts at about 2100°F. (1149°C.). This is within the raku temperature range, but not comfortably so; after 2100°F., a more refractory material must be used. Red brick cannot stand heat fluctuation, and the ability to withstand this is crucial in a raku kiln; red brick responds to fluctuation by spalling and cracking.

It is not advisable to discount red bricks entirely, however, because they can be used for low temperature firing, and can certainly be recommended as a secondary or outside layer on a kiln. They are reasonably heavy (this can be an advantage in construction: for example, in corbeled arch kilns). They are readily available, and cheap.

Hard Firebrick. Hard firebricks are made of fireclay and kaolin, and therefore have high refractory properties. They are hard and dense with a relatively stable volume.

Resistance to cracking and spalling is a property of hard firebrick. It weathers well, and absorbs less moisture than soft firebrick. It is resistant to wear and abrasion, fatigue resistant, and is a relatively good insulator. So widely is it used, that it is available almost everywhere and is much cheaper than soft firebrick. Its high heat retention allows rapid firing cycles.

The potential disadvantages of hard firebrick center around this high heat retention; it takes a long time to heat a kiln built of them to the required temperature, which results in a large expenditure of fuel and a consequent increase in costs. However, this may be compensated for by shorter subsequent firings. Also, as mentioned before, it is not advisable to put a cold, large piece into such a hot chamber provided by the high capacity of heat retention of these bricks. Sometimes, though, this problem can be avoided by preheating the pots on the kiln top. To build a removable door out of hard firebrick is not advisable either, as they are too heavy to lift with ease, and would be too hot to touch. A newly opened kiln blasts out a lot of heat, and the intensity would be much greater with hard firebrick than with any other. The potter's comfort and even safety is therefore a factor.

Hard firebrick can be used for the kiln chamber while a lighter brick can be used to build the removable door.

Soft or Insulation Brick. Soft or insulation bricks are made from refractory fire clay and kaolin, reduced to slip, and then aerated chemically. They are fired in large volumes and then cut when cool into exact brick shapes. The dimensions are therefore more precise than those of hard bricks which are molded as slip, and naturally shrink slightly in the firing.

Various grades of soft firebrick are available, the refractory level being indicated by K or G factors. K or G plus a number means that the brick can be used up to a temperature of 100 times that number, e.g., K23 bricks are good to 2300°F. (1260°C.), K26 bricks are good to 2600°F. (1427°C.), and so on. The cost of each brick increases with the K number. We recommend K23 refractories, although K20 or K26 may be more economical or appropriate, depending on the firing temperature expected.

A high resistance to heat comprises the main advantage of soft firebrick. Because the soft firebricks throw the heat into the kiln, less heat is lost or stored in the bricks, and consequently much fuel is saved. However, this advantage is reduced in raku because the chamber is continually being opened and closed, thus allowing heat to escape.

Insulating bricks are light and easy to build with; they are also soft enough to cut with an old wood-cutting saw,

Nancy Jurs drilled holes in the soft insulation brick and inserted solid metal rods to be able to remove the door of her kiln easily in three separate pieces. As shown, there is a tendency for the soft brick to crack near the rod.

or to drill holes in for construction purposes. They do not deteriorate fast under constant heating and cooling, and, in fact, insulate so well that a kiln roof of the thickness of a single brick will remain quite cool on the outside. The kiln can be put indoors without great discomfort from sheer heat, and heat dissipates from the chamber relatively quickly, which can sometimes be an advantage. While, for these reasons, most raku potters prefer to use insulation bricks for their glaze kiln, there are disadvantages to them which must also be mentioned. They do not withstand weather well, and if the kiln is to be outside it must be protected from rain and dampness. The softness of the bricks, which is the source of their main advantages, also means that they can crack and crumble under physical stress. The kiln must be designed and built carefully, and must not rely on the sheer strength of materials for its solidity. The inevitable financial loss from cracking, and they do tend to crack easily, must be offset against the possible fuel savings gained with these bricks. These bricks require particular care when cutting and assembling them.

Soft firebricks are not as readily available as other kinds, and are very expensive to buy. Most brickyards, however, and big companies such as A. P. Green and Harbison Walker will be able to supply them (see Suppliers List). Their main advantage is their light weight which makes them easily portable. In the long run, however, they disintegrate, and the potter is left with refractory material which can be used in casting refractory materials, as described in the following section.

Castable Refractories. Good as bricks are for many construction tasks, there are special cases where it is more advisable to go to a different material. Castable refractories were first used as an alternative to brick in commercial smelters in the steel industry, or for similar purposes.

In general, the use of castable materials in raku kilns can be an advantage in cases where the kiln is unusually large or of a peculiar shape, the castable mix simply being poured into the required forms. Some or all parts of the kiln can be constructed in this way. If the kiln is of an ordinary design, but will be exposed to extreme weather, it might be better to construct it out of a castable refractory material, as it withstands such harsh conditions better than most brick.

Yet another advantage to castables is that crumbled insulation brick which seems useless can be incorporated into the refractory mix, provided that the fragments can be rendered small enough.

If, however, you are a potter who continually rebuilds your kiln according to the changing needs of your pots, then the relative permanence of castables can be a disadvantage.

Most refractory companies put out a line of several different kinds of castables, all of which serve special requirements and are worth investigating, but most are ex-
pensive. There are mixes, however, which the potter can make very easily. Homemade castables can be made with crushed soft insulation brick, grog, combustible material such as leaves or sawdust (these will burn out and leave insulating air pockets), combined with vermiculite or a bonding cement. Depending on the castable you mix up, the forms can be dried and used or they can be fired in another kiln to provide extra strength and heat durability. Usually Portland cement is not used if the cast pieces are to be fired in a kiln before being used for building. Calcium alumina cement, however, can withstand red heat and is the cement most often used in these cases. A mixture using vermiculite can also be fired prior to use.

Wooden forms are prepared for the kiln size or sections you need. After adding water to the chosen formula so that it is plastic but does not flow, the mixture is rammed tightly into the forms. When the mixture has set for a few hours, the forms can be removed carefully and the resulting shape should be left for a few days to cure. Then the shapes should be fired, if necessary. Later the cast shapes can be incorporated into the kiln structure.

Fiberfrax Lo-Con Felt. Although Fiberfrax Lo-Con felt is a relatively new insulating material, it is gaining widespread use among raku potters. It is made from alumina silica fibers with honeycomb structures. Manufactured by the Carborundum Company (see Suppliers List), it is sold in rolls and is easily cut. The most common size is a density of 6 lbs. per cu. ft.

Most Fibrefrax kilns for raku use large metal oil drums for the supporting framework. These drums have to be sufficiently cleaned (sandblasted) inside, and are cut down to the required height. The Lo-Con felt is glued to the inside with a special glue: QF-180, also manufactured by Carborundum.[1]

Lo-Con felt is lightweight and therefore most kilns made with it are portable and easy to handle. The material will withstand the raku temperature range and conserves more fuel than some kinds of brick. Large raku kilns can be quickly constructed, provided that a suitable structure, such as a metal drum, can be found to support the felt.

Once the Fiberfrax is glued onto the drum, or whatever the framework may be, it is more or less fixed there permanently, until the material wears out. It cannot easily be removed and reused. Using Fiberfrax, therefore, fixes the size and shape of the particular kiln built with it, and this might be a disadvantage, depending on the range of pots you are likely to be making. In debating about the choice of Fiberfrax, the potter has to decide whether the initial cost is worth the amount of use he expects to get from the kiln. Fiberfrax varies in cost depending on the density and thickness of the piece.

Kiln Shelves. A kiln shelf of some kind may be required. It may be supported by pottery posts or by firebrick. Shelves made of silicon carbide are expensive and are

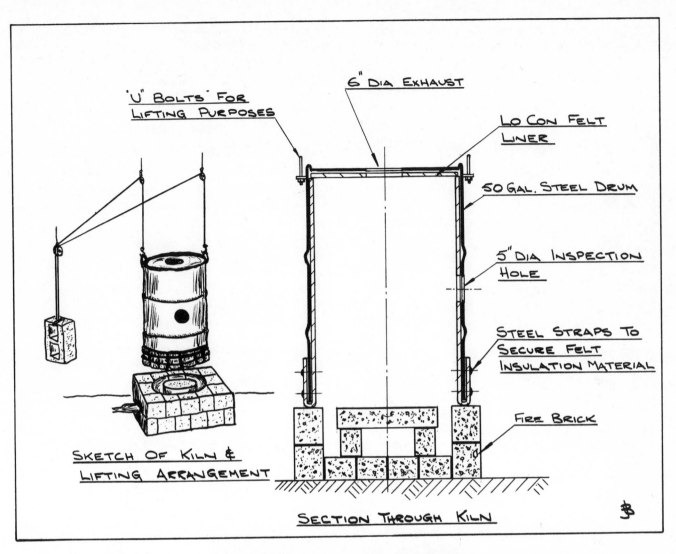

6" DIA EXHAUST

LO CON FELT LINER

50 GAL. STEEL DRUM

5" DIA INSPECTION HOLE

STEEL STRAPS TO SECURE FELT INSULATION MATERIAL

FIRE BRICK

'U' BOLTS' FOR LIFTING PURPOSES

SKETCH OF KILN & LIFTING ARRANGEMENT

SECTION THROUGH KILN

Diagram of a lift-off barrel kiln.

Part of the construction of a small drum kiln made from Lo-Con felt. The drum is placed on bricks and a hole cut for the single burner port.

An experimental raku kiln built and designed by Henry Gernhardt. The kiln is made of Kaowool attached to a 1/8" (3mm) asbestos board box frame. The kiln is lightweight, radiates little heat, and is easily transported.

liable to crack in the conditions imposed by a raku firing. Cheaper, fire-clay shelves are recommended and any used, chipped, or cracked one will do. The rule is to use whatever rejects are practicable. Spilled glaze should be removed and the shelf cleaned and coated with kiln wash before use.

Burners

Before choosing the type of burners necessary for a raku kiln, several factors should be taken into consideration: the fuel you want to use, the design and size of the kiln, its site, the temperature range, the kind of firing, and, of course, the cost. The design of the burners and the necessary equipment will depend most of all on the choice of fuel.

Hoses and Regulator for Gas. Propane and natural gas fittings are generally interchangeable. Most welding supply companies can furnish all the necessary hoses and fittings.

Oil Burners. Oil as a liquid burns sluggishly, giving off little heat. The principle behind oil burners is the conversion of the liquid into a vapor. The burner breaks up the liquid into tiny drops and mixes air with them; this mixture is then ignited. The common types of oil burners are *vaporizing, high-pressure, rotary,* and *low-pressure.*

The *vaporizing oil burner* works on the principle of changing the physical state of oil from a liquid into a gas for combustion. In this type of burner, the oil flow is measured and metered before it is supplied to the vaporizer. Oil flows into the burner and is ignited as a liquid. Then vaporization takes place. Oil vapor rises in the burner, combining with the air which enters through air ports. These ports are evenly spaced and of a given size. The fuel-vapor mixture continues to rise and absorb more air until the correct quantity of air has combined with the oil vapor. At this point, the combustion process is functioning completely.

In pottery, and especially for raku firing, *low-pressure burners* are most often used. Some low-pressure oil burners use a fuel pump and mix air and oil within the burner

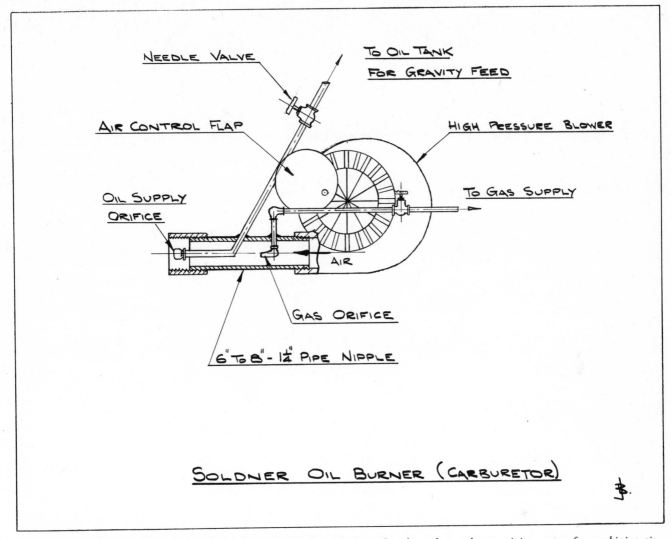

NEEDLE VALVE

TO OIL TANK
FOR GRAVITY FEED

AIR CONTROL FLAP

HIGH PRESSURE BLOWER

OIL SUPPLY
ORIFICE

TO GAS SUPPLY

AIR

GAS ORIFICE

6" TO 8" - 1¼" PIPE NIPPLE

SOLDNER OIL BURNER (CARBURETOR)

Diagram of the Soldner oil "carburetor." Soldner calls this a carburetor rather than a burner because it is a system for combining air and fuel with no combustion actually taking place inside the device.

nozzle itself. The mixture is sprayed in vapor form into the firebox. Combustion takes place within the firebox itself. For burners using forced air or a fuel pump, a supply of electricity is required to run these motors.

There is no need for a very complex oil burner for raku. Commercial ones are usually both expensive and needlessly efficient for small raku kilns. Moreover, such efficiency is sometimes harmful to the ware. Homemade oil burners can be made from supplies similar to those suggested in the following section for natural gas and propane. Instead of a fuel pump, gravity can be utilized. Oil, however, requires a long fuel line (about 15′, 4.6m) in order to keep the oil tank a safe distance from the burners.

The kiln is very much part of the burner system. Paul Soldner calls the burners "carburetors," because they are only a mixing device for the air and fuel. Combustion does not take place here, but in the kiln chamber itself. According to this view a "burner system," of which the kiln is an important part, is the proper description of the whole apparatus for firing with oil.

Natural Gas and Propane Burners. For their operation at raku temperatures, natural gas and propane burners are essentially the same in principle and design. Since the termperature range of raku is fairly low, these burners need not be too complex—in fact, the simpler they are, the better. While burners of all types should work efficiently, sometimes they can burn too hot and this is just as undesirable as those that will not reach the desired temperature. Basically, there are two categories for burners using natural gas and propane. These are *atmospheric* or *inspirating* burners, and *forced air burners.*

Atmospheric burners are the simplest and most easily constructed. They require the least amount of equipment and are usually the most portable. Burners of this type can be constructed out of regular plumbing supplies. Black iron is most often used. Commercial burners are sold as either "weed burners" or "Tigertorches." Both make use of the venturi principle, having long tubes that widen progressively toward the exhaust end. Because the tube is narrow where the gas enters and widens later,

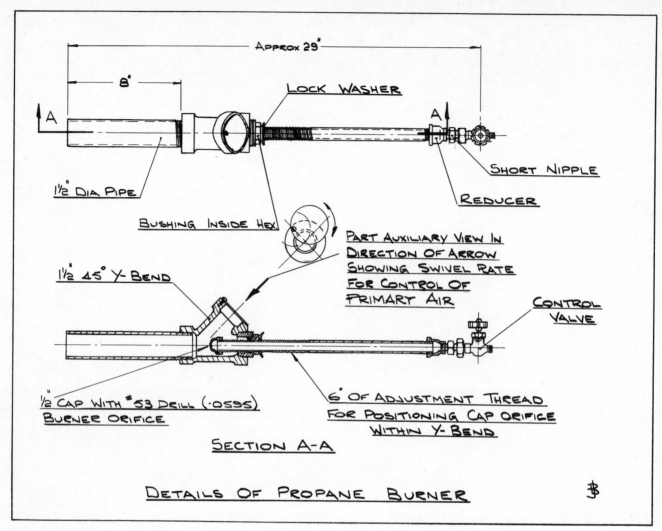

APPROX 29"

8"

A

LOCK WASHER

A

SHORT NIPPLE

REDUCER

1½" DIA PIPE

BUSHING INSIDE HEX

PART AUXILIARY VIEW IN
DIRECTION OF ARROW
SHOWING SWIVEL RATE
FOR CONTROL OF
PRIMART AIR

1½" 45° Y-BEND

CONTROL
VALVE

½" CAP WITH #53 DRILL (·0595)
BURNER ORIFICE

6" OF ADJUSTMENT THREAD
FOR POSITIONING CAP ORIFICE
WITHIN Y-BEND

SECTION A-A

DETAILS OF PROPANE BURNER

Diagram of raku burners made from simple plumbing supplies—in this case a large Y and a pipe nipple 1 1/2" x 8" (3.8 x 20.3 cm), with a 1/2" (12.7 mm) diameter black pipe. The primary air enters the Y and secondary air is drawn in at the burner port.

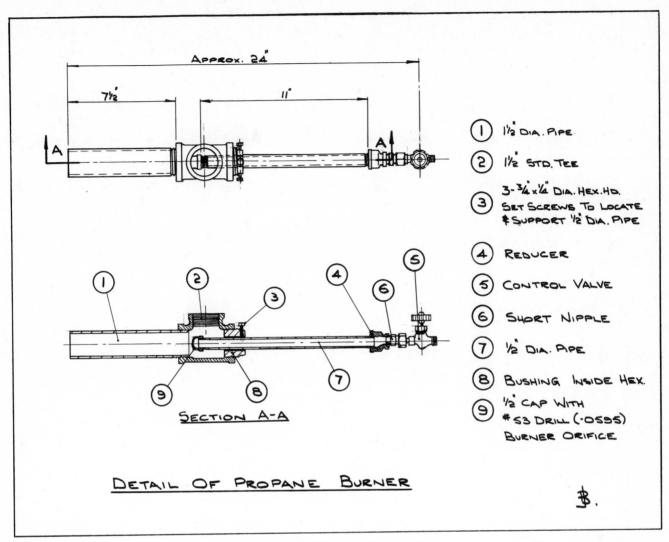

APPROX. 24"

7½"

11"

A

A

① 1½" DIA. PIPE.

② 1½" STD. TEE

③ 3-¾" x ¼" DIA. HEX.HD.
SET SCREWS TO LOCATE
& SUPPORT ½" DIA. PIPE

④ REDUCER

⑤ CONTROL VALVE

⑥ SHORT NIPPLE

⑦ ½" DIA. PIPE

⑧ BUSHING INSIDE HEX.

⑨ ½" CAP WITH
53 DRILL (·0595)
BURNER ORIFICE

SECTION A-A

DETAIL OF PROPANE BURNER

Diagram of an alternative atmospheric propane burner made from plumbing supplies.

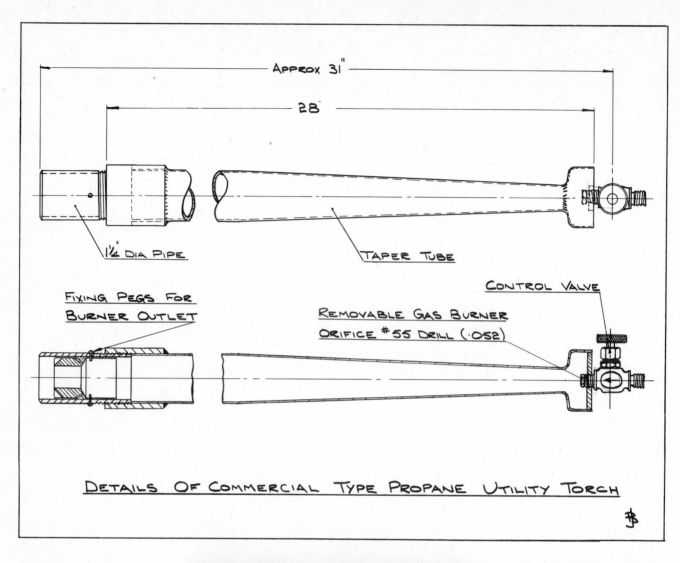

APPROX 31"

28"

1¼" DIA PIPE

TAPER TUBE

FIXING PEGS FOR
BURNER OUTLET

CONTROL VALVE

REMOVABLE GAS BURNER
ORIFICE #55 DRILL (·052)

DETAILS OF COMMERCIAL TYPE PROPANE UTILITY TORCH

Diagram of a commercial weed burner or Tigertorch which uses the venturi principle.

Propane burners designed and built by John Frisenda for his Fiberfrax kiln. The holes in the pipe nipple provide the primary air source.

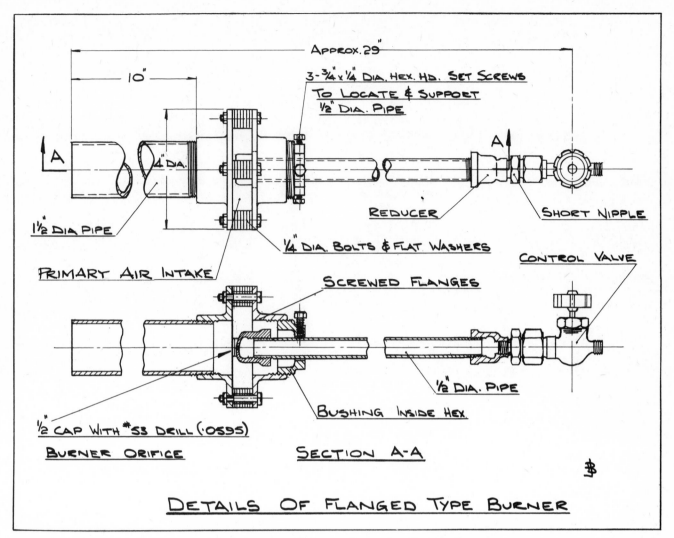

Approx. 29"

10"

3-¾" x ¼" Dia. Hex. Hd. Set Screws
To Locate & Support
½" Dia. Pipe

A

A

4" Dia.

1½" Dia Pipe

Reducer

Short Nipple

¼" Dia. Bolts & Flat Washers

Primary Air Intake

Screwed Flanges

Control Valve

½" Dia. Pipe

Bushing Inside Hex

½" Cap With #53 Drill (.0595)

Burner Orifice

Section A-A

Details Of Flanged Type Burner

Diagram of a homemade propane atmospheric burner made from ordinary plumbing supplies.

there is a vacuum in the tube when gas passes through. A small quantity of air is drawn into the burners through an air opening behind the orifice which introduces gas into the burner tube. The size of the air opening should be large enough to burn the fuel sufficiently. The end of the tube usually has a heat-resistant tip.

Homemade atmospheric burners can use regular plumbing fixtures such as large Ys and Ts for the primary source of air. Secondary air is drawn in at the burner ports where they pierce the kiln wall.

The main difference between atmospheric burners that use propane or natural gas is the size of the orifice. Since propane is bottled under tremendous pressure, the orifice size of the burner will be much smaller than that for natural gas. When making your own atmospheric burners, two major considerations are the orifice size and the primary air supply. As a general rule, the orifice should be positioned just ahead of the primary air supply. If the orifice size is too large or too small in proportion to the amount of primary air, the burner may be inefficient and not be able to reach temperature. Either there will be too much unburnt fuel, causing a reduction atmosphere, or too little fuel to create the necessary energy. If the orifice size is too large with a correspondingly large primary air supply, this can burn too hot, causing problems in the ware, such as sudden overfiring, cracking, or explosions.

These are some considerations that have to be made when constructing your own burners. Usually with a new burner set-up, a trial and error period is necessary, when the right adjustments to the orifice size, primary air capacity, tube length, etc. can be made. Raku burners can be designed to control the atmosphere desired in the kiln for a variety of glaze effects in raku firing.

Forced Air Burners. These burners are more efficient than atmospheric burners, largely because there is more control over the gas-air mixture. This control and efficiency allows a rapid firing cycle. Usually, these kinds of burners are not needed for raku temperatures, but if you have this kind of burner and want to use it for raku, natural gas is generally used, because of its pressure being lower than propane. Commercial burners of this type are expensive and have too much potential that will remain unused in raku. To cut the cost, a vacuum cleaner could be adapted to a homemade atmospheric burner, with a change in the orifice size to create sufficient forced air for raku temperatures.

Along with both atmospheric and forced air burners, some equipment is necessary. For propane, a high-pressure tank regulator and high-pressure rubber hoses are needed to hook up the burners to the fuel supply. The use of a brass Y connection is needed if two burners are being used. Small brass needle valves near the burner orifice can give independent control over each burner.

With the use of natural gas, a meter that is connected to the main supply is required.

A consideration of all the demands of the potter's situation will often make the choice of kiln type and equipment fairly easy and logical.

A commercial weed burner (Manchester Grass Burner Torch) used by Sister Mary Bourke for her roll-out kiln.

With fuel shortages a real concern, potters are designing kilns with new alternatives. This kiln was designed by Paul Soldner and makes use of solar energy. It is highly experimental and not necessarily to be used for raku.

A smoky atmosphere, permeating clothes and hair: Dave Tell at work.

6

Firing and Post-Firing

Flame. Burners roaring. Fear and enforced patience. Trial . . .

Pots incandescent, descend, decanted like glowing wine into barrels of smoky dust. Glowing faces glimpsed through smoke.

The images and feelings of raku firing are climactic.

The potter's efforts culminate in the glaze firing and the post-firing of raku. The hours of work and thought are to be tested, and the pots transformed, by the arbitrary and capricious behavior of the materials and process. Fire-formed, the pots can only be partially altered by the action of the potter; smoke-changed, the ashes fall from them as from the phoenix.

The process of creation in raku is extended into the firing and post-firing, yet this time is one of extremes, for the pots can be either destroyed or reanimated by the flames. This final stage seems, in its closeness to disaster or success, to participate in other vital human events, like birth or death. A raku firing is like a live performance of improvised music or dance: the overall form and feeling have been explored and rehearsed, the instruments tuned, but much depends on the congruity of minds and medium. Above all, success depends on the synthesis of the planned and the unforeseen to produce a statement whose creative source is unfathomable.

A raku pot is completely formed only when it has come through the test of fire and the difficulties of improvisation, and is cold. The creative influence of the raku potter over his pot is extended, but its success depends on split-second decisions. This extension, however, increases the chances of disaster as well as success. How can the potter prepare himself? What are the equivalents in raku to rehearsals in the performing arts? How can the potter maintain control over his situation?

Simply put, the answer to these questions is that the potter cannot be afraid of making decisions, for throughout the many stages which a raku pot undergoes, the potter must decide many times. His control at each stage is extended by an understanding and recall of the earlier stages and his decisions are informed accordingly, not only during the forming and glazing, as is usual with all ceramic processes, but also during the firing and post-firing. A growing familiarity with the behavior of materials in response to his ideas and to physical forces should lead to more controlled pots. By the post-firing stage, the potter should know what has happened to each pot up to that point, and he should know what he still wants to do with it. At the same time, raku is a chancy thing. The processes of chance should be followed through and not suppressed, as might be the case if the potter overplans or is not prepared to change his mind according to a swift intuition or hunch. Risks are part of the process, and disasters sometimes the result. In a curious way, though, failures in firing tend to integrate the philosophy of the whole process.

To face the possibility of the negation of an idea by the operations of chance in the firing is one of the hardest things in raku. While experience can alleviate some mistakes and the potter can learn in many ways, firing remains a testing time for the potter's character as well as for his pots. It is a trial for his perseverance, and for his ability to risk his intuitions and his judgment.

Control

A newcomer to raku, if he were unexpectedly to see a raku firing, might ask what is so difficult, so "artistic" about this? Where is the control, the organization, the professionalism? And certainly, compared to the sight of a big, indoor electric or oil-fired kiln, replete with all the dials, switches, pipes, and hardware of an advanced technology, raku looks slapdash indeed. Yet it is not.

In a general sense, it could be said that there are two types of pottery: that in which accurate prediction of effects plays a great part, such as in multifired luster ware, and that which allows for accidents, such as salt glazing, wood firing, or raku. Control and artistry need not be absent from the latter types, just because accidents are allowed to happen. The different kind of control results from a different attitude to clay, to the process, to oneself, and even to life. This attitude in raku involves the acceptance of certain unintended effects and unforeseen possibilities creatively. Raku can magnify that cooperation and improvisation between artist and material which must exist in any medium. The raku potter may need as part of his intellectual equipment a creative acceptance of, and openness to, effects beyond the scope of his intention—fully realizing this is a form of preparation.

Speed is inherent in all aspects of the process—the firing is usually short and the activities in post-firing are often frenzied; it requires a certain kind of control, and an exact adjustment of mind to the rapid and apparently random procedure. It needs speed, coordination, physical guts, and teamwork. The long tongs demand experience and skill, for it is easy to drop a pot, or to scar the glaze badly, though competent scars can be a signature of the process. To take pots from a red-hot kiln takes courage. The heat is intense; often, a big pot has to be lifted out of the kiln with hands protected only by asbestos gloves. The reaching into the kiln has to be controlled and decisive. Other people involved in the firing have to be cooperative and experienced, with their roles assigned. Practice in these aspects of raku can give a measure of control.

Even inside the kiln, all is not left to the inscrutable kiln god. The contact with the pot is as direct as possible. The potter checks the glaze melt by eye and can decide, using the accuracy of experience, when to take out the pot with a correctly matured glaze or whether to underfire or overfire it. He can regulate the kiln to produce an oxidizing atmosphere or one of partial reduction. He need not smoke the pot, but if he does he can lay the pot down at a particular angle, smoke all of it, or part. A selection of the combustible material for the post-firing has to be made. The choices, in fact, are legion. In the rapid exercise of choice itself, and of course in his finesse in carrying it out, lies the raku potter's control.

This control, however, does not disguise the paradox that the potter should know by experience what his choice will lead to, yet he can never know beforehand the exact results.

In writing of prediction and control in raku, one is reminded of W. H. Auden's comments on meaning in poetry: "How can I know what I think," he asked, "till I see what I say?" Often, the raku potter will proceed with the conviction that he is doing a particular thing and, by rapidly assessing the effect of unexpected results, can create a pot that is the result of his making, yet greater than he made.

Common Sense Preparations

Because the events of firing and post-firing are so rapid, it is helpful to make whatever physical arrangements are possible beforehand, besides making the attitudinal ones already mentioned. Following are some practical suggestions.

Glazing. Preferably, the pots should be glazed a few days in advance so that they can dry out completely. A damp pot placed in a hot kiln will probably crack or explode. Pots freshly glazed can sometimes be dried sufficiently by being placed on the top of the warm kiln during the earlier firings.

Kiln Area. Prepare the general area around the kiln according to what you know is going to happen. It is inadvisable to work in a confined space.

Kiln Interior. Check the shelves to see that there is no glaze on them—otherwise the pots can stick to the shelf. If the kiln bricks are wet, preheat the kiln gently to drive off moisture.

Loading. If there is to be more than one pot in the kiln, remember that the pot nearest to the door is most likely to come out first, and will be the hottest. Pots are likely to react more to a reduction atmosphere the hotter they are, and should be loaded accordingly, bearing in mind the design of the kiln, and the relative position of the door and the burners. There are many variations of post-firing effects which depend just on the heat of the pot and therefore indirectly affect the order in which the pots are loaded. Some potters keep the burners on after the glazes have matured, but turned down, so that the pots nearest to them do not cool down so quickly, and the burners do not have to be relit constantly.

Fuel. Make sure that you have more than enough fuel. An interrupted firing can be costly and disappointing. If using oil or gas as a fuel, check all connections for leaks.

Safety. Since you will be looking directly at the pots in the kiln, your face and eyes may need to be shielded. Long hair should be tied back. When removing pots from the kiln, use tongs or wear asbestos gloves and long sleeves. Always use common sense as a guideline for safety.

Firing. The details of the firing procedure itself vary according to the design of the kiln and on the choice of fuel. For details related to these points, see Chapter 5: Kilns—Requirements, Construction, and Use.

Judging the Glaze Melt

It is impossible to describe or photograph what a raku glaze looks like when it is properly melted—indeed there

George and Betty Woodman (above) work together
in the firing and post-firing.

Nancy Baldwin washing a pot
after it has been cooled in sand.

Paul Soldner pulling a pot from his kiln.

is no "proper" melt, as a certain effect may require underfiring or overfiring. Also, a raku firing is so fast that a perfectly even glaze melt does not always take place. However, there are standard stages which quickly become easy to recognize:

1. The glaze changes into a hard crust. Then it gets just a little shiny.

2. As the heat increases, the fluxes in the glaze begin to work and bubbles and small blisters appear on the side of the pot.

3. Next, the bubbles open and disappear and different parts of the glaze flow at different times.

4. Gradually, the whole surface of the pot becomes reflective and glossy, to a degree depending on the glaze. This is usually the final stage.

5. Sometimes dark bubbles and pits stay on the surface. In this case keep firing and let the heat soak in without increasing the temperature. If the glaze surface appears to be erupting (boiling), then overfiring has begun or there is too much unburnt fuel and consequently harsh reduction inside the kiln. To prevent the glaze from volatizing further, you can turn the fuel supply down and the glaze might smooth out. Look at the pot at an angle, so you can see the light reflected.

6. When you decide the glaze is ready—usually when the surface apppears to have an even, glossy texture—decrease the heat and quickly begin your post-firing procedure.

Post-Firing

For a raku firing to be understood, the factual knowledge and the experience itself must coalesce. The novice, seeing a raku firing for the first time, might turn away; or he might stay, fascinated, as many people are. In either case he probably could not be expected to understand the complexities underneath the apparently casual activities of the craftsmen during the firing. They talk and joke, but are nevertheless busy with their thoughts. The potter is probably thinking of the pots in the kiln, running his mind over their forms, their characteristics. He is probably thinking also of his alternatives in post-firing, though he may not arrange them systematically in his mind at this late stage. A person anxious to know more about raku post-firing might best do so by putting himself in the place of this hypothetical potter, who is waiting for the glaze to melt, and thinking of what he can do.

The potter may recheck the area around him. Are the combustibles close at hand, will he trip over anything or anyone, and do the helpers know what he's going to do?

He may think about how he is going to remove the pot from the kiln. Unless part of the kiln moves, allowing him to treat the pot where it stands, he may have to use tongs or just gloved hands. If he uses tongs, he will have to

Dave Tell begins a firing.

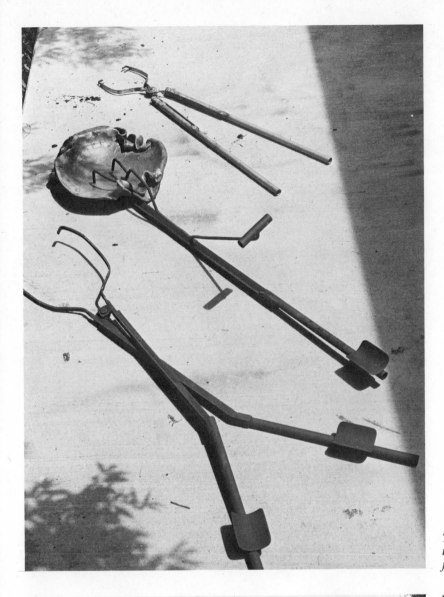

Tongs owned by Nancy Jurs that were designed specifically for the kind of pots she makes.

Nancy Jurs demonstrating the use of large tongs for a pot to be reduced in leaves.

Henry Gernhardt removing a pot from the kiln to begin the post-firing process. The post-firing materials are conveniently placed; he and his assistant coordinate their efforts.

Reducing.

Quenching.

For the next pot, Henry prepares a different reduction container while the pot is being fired. The post-firing process made the potter search for different materials for reduction. Here he is using ticker-tape.

think about whether or not he wants tong marks on the pot, and where they should be if he does. If he does not want the marks, he will have to pick up the pot by an unglazed area or fire it hot enough that the glaze will heal over immediately, or alternatively let the pot cool in the kiln. He will, of course, have already checked that the tongs are big enough to pick up the pot.

He may also check the weather. If a harsh wind is blowing, the work area should be shielded somehow, as smoke can be uncontrollable, or the pots can crack from cooling too fast. Rain or snow, and excessive cold can all affect the procedures.

The temperature of the pot when it is pulled out is important. The hotter the pot, the more reduction, the blacker the clay from smoke, the more chances of lustrous effects. Certain glazes, particularly copper-bearing ones, should be partially reduced in the kiln, taken out at the top of the heat, and post-reduced with utmost speed. If the pot glazed with a copper glaze looks green in color when it's brought out of the kiln, it has begun to reoxidize, and will be difficult to reduce in the post-firing.

The potter may check his combustible materials, to see whether they are dry. If they are not, intense smoke will not result because the heat from the pot is being used to drive off the steam from the combustibles. For lots of reduction and a lot of smoke, sawdust is the best combustible. While straw or hay is good for other effects, in large quantities it can explode into flames so quickly that the potter may not be able to get near the pot to work with it. Newspaper burns too quickly and doesn't reduce for very long. However, anything soaked with oil will give a lot of smoke. The potter may check in his mind that he has the right material for the effects he wants on the pots now being fired. Also, his reducing containers, such as garbage cans with lids, should be ready. On the other hand, he may choose to reduce without containers, partially burying his pot in combustibles, and partially exposing it to the air. This gives him more varied surface effects and some control over where the effects take place, but increases the risk of cracking the pot. When running over some of the procedures in his mind, the potter must prepare to use patience to resist looking at a pot on which he wants complete reduction while it is in its container. To be safe, it should be sealed away from the air without interruption for about 30 minutes, despite temptations to see how it is doing!

If he wants a pot to crackle, the potter must be prepared to stay with the pot. Crazing does not happen immediately. He must force it to craze, cooling it, exposing it to air, until it begins to make pinging sounds as it begins to craze and may be smoked to create crackle. Sawdust is best for control of crackle—it is easy to place on a specific area of a pot and burns for a long time. There should be a good supply of it as it is sometimes necessary to add more to the pot.

As the time of the melt approaches, the potter may rehearse in his mind the steps he is going to take. He may not think just of the technical aspects of the post-firing, for other aspects are just as important; he may be readying himself psychologically. He may worry whether the people working with him will anticipate what he wants. He may grow frightened of the heat, of reaching into the red-hot kiln, of singeing eyelashes, hair, of the heat reddening his face. As the time for action grows closer, his thoughts may coalesce, becoming less systematic and separated, becoming more feelings than thoughts, more anticipated reactions than plans. As the door is unbricked, he just hopes he guesses right.

In the haste that follows, he does not always think; most of the time he acts, reacts, dances with his glowing partners, turning to place them gently, the roaring of the burners still in his ears. "This pot needs to be oxidized. This pot partly reduced. This pot . . ."

A pot on its side. A swelling form in sawdust. The flames lick its side, soft flames, licking like a cat taking the fog from its coat; soft shapes, tongues which curl with rasping heat, which immolate. A coalescence of softness and harshness.

Another pot grays to carbon black. Sawdust sprinkled from the tips of the fingers like seeds into the earth. The clay sprouts tiny flames, harsh and soft.

Another loading. The cycle begins again. Thoughts turn, steady and moving. A quiet beginning to the rhythm of another firing. The heat builds. "Turn up the burners."

Pink.

Orange.

The melt! The melt! Empty, release the pots. "This one reduce completely. Straw or hay this time. Ram down that bucket there. Fine." This one must be black, black. "Lift that cover. Flash it. Good." The final pot, brought out last of all, is air-cooling on the kiln top. As the sounds die down—the burners are off, the flames slowed, and the buckets no longer rattle—all the pots join it in giving off small sounds. The soft pings of crazing are quiet bells like echoes in a cave, minimal sounds quietly delineating silence all the more.

The paradox of sound and silence, of harshness and softness. He feels exhausted, relaxed, contented. "It's not bad." The potter shakes his head. "Though I'm disappointed about that round one."

In thinking about it later, the post-firing procedure seems to include an element of dance. The checking of the melt, the removal of the door with a swing of the body, the lifting of the pot and its placement in sawdust while people cross and recross from kiln to regulator, from door to sawdust, form a kind of functional choreography which is never quite repeated. The dance may not be a primarily decorative one in itself, but certain movements are the same, and there is always a relationship between them. Physical coordination and teamwork, mental preparedness and agility, purposeful

Raku Jar *by Howard Yana-Shapiro. 16" (40.6 cm) high. Thrown and smoked to stain the crackle.*

Raku Vessel *by Richard Hirsch. 28" (71.1 cm) high. Thrown, slabbed, and incised. Unglazed, smoked with straw resist to form a negative pattern.*

movements in time, are all recorded on the pot.

As with pots at the end of any firing, all that remains to be done is to scrub off the residue and excess results of the procedure and observe the clean, finished statements.

Concentration and Simplicity

We have given many possibilities to define a happening that can be, essentially and in the best sense, a simple one. Perhaps the preceding pages have added another dimension to the firing scene viewed by the newcomer. To the person experienced in raku, the unobtrusive nature of the firing, the apparent disorder, the lack of equipment, and the casualness spell human interaction, the apparently thoughtless motions indicate thought too fast to detail. It is difficult to learn about post-firing except by direct experience. Because of this aspect of its nature, the tendency to make a public party out of raku can be harmful—at least to the pots produced in this way, for the potter needs a minimum of distraction and a few friends who know the routine, and who can sense the urgencies before being told. Sometimes what the potter needs is just to be by himself with his pots and his kiln.

So many different effects can be obtained as a result of the firing, that it is a time of concentration and mental effort. The firing is the most public and the most publicized aspect of raku, but, in a sense, the raku firing cannot be adequately demonstrated by anyone. If one is concentrating on the demonstration, it is more difficult to focus on the pots themselves. As the pots become more sophisticated there may be too much to think about to explain to an audience what is happening, and the explanation will not fit the event. Students, sometimes not realizing fully the importance of firing and post-firing, may allow someone else to fire their pots for them, as is often done with stoneware, and an entire kiln load of various people's pots may be treated in the same way. However, the advantage of raku is that each pot can have individual post-firing treatment, and this should be done as an integral part of the creative process by the person who made the pot.

A raku firing should be neither routine nor entertainment. The intense but relaxed atmosphere of a well-conducted firing should exude the easy contentment that is part of the original meaning of the word "raku."

In this book, we have tried to indicate the range of possibilities in post-firing, but one result of greater experience will probably be the need to deliberately limit surface effects. The novice often gets a smattering of everything on his raku pot—partial reduction, smoked raw clay, metallic luster, lots of crackle. A familiarity with all the possible effects may induce the potter to do them more justice by exploring each one further and by eliminating some on each pot to concentrate on others. Finding precedent in Piet Mondrian's search for simplification or in that of the Japanese originators of the raku

Weatherscape . . . Farm Country Plate by Art Haney. Thrown, raku luster. An example of a departure from standard techniques, this plate incorporates multi-firing, commercial luster, cone 06–04 frit glazes, rapid cooling in the electric kiln, and finally, smoking.

process, the potter discovers that control through simplicity is the tradition of process and design in art.

Conclusions

The raku pot is the record of how the potter reacts to a certain process: his openness to events, his speed of reaction, and his ability to make finished statements out of fleeting moments of time. Also involved is his skill and knowledge of the process, and his finesse in execution. Above all, as the rapid events of post-firing unfold in the cooling pot which changes as he watches, what probably counts most is his creative acceptance of random effects.

Facing the loss of an idea which the destruction or failure of a raku pot entails is difficult, but the loss need not necessarily be total, for some potters work in a series, producing alternative forms and nuances of expression encompassed in one idea. Provided that the basic idea is fertile and strong enough, there need be no repetition. To submit such a series to the raku firing process is possibly an expansion of the raku attitude. As the potter's ideas grow, so must the process.

When Paul Soldner in 1960 reduced a pot in a gutter full of pepper leaves he was expanding a process which, though it utilized chance to some extent and expressed an acceptance of the irregular, had not changed for nearly 400 years. Soldner's discovery is typical of what can happen in modern raku in his response to what he saw, and in his use both of theoretical knowledge and handy materials. Yet Soldner's method is typical also in that it cannot be repeated too often. Just as a raku pot can evolve as the potter responds to events, so too can the raku process evolve *as a process.* As potters observe the unexpected successes of certain actions, they will probably want to apply what has been discovered, thereby extending the process even farther. Soldner's discovery defined raku as a process capable of evolution and change. The challenge now to each potter working in the medium is to understand and carry out the possibilities inherent at each stage, and, by extending the process, produce vital pots.

A Real Raku Get-Together.
*A Soldner workshop in full swing
shows much activity
and group involvement.*

Platter *by Jun Kaneko. 13 1/2" x 13" (34.2 x 33 cm). 1971. Kaneko, a Japanese potter now living in the United States, shows in this piece the absorption of both the traditional and Western approaches to raku.*

The Nature of Raku

The technique of raku is usually thought of as firing at low temperatures, sometimes but not always, removing the pot form from the kiln while red hot and, sometimes smoking . . . or reducing . . . it to develop the desired effect. However, this is only the physical aspect of the work and does not include the attitude or philosophy of the artist, or the decorating and handling which is the result of this. Although the result is called 'raku,' it is related to the Japanese tradition only in incept in that it offers our western culture insight into oriental concepts of beauty: Ideally, and what is striven to attain, is the incorporation of a masterful command of asymmetric balance in design, a highly developed tactile sensibility in appreciation of materials, and a virtuosity of decorative techniques into a unified whole . . . the overall effect of which is a spontaneously achieved finished work. As done in America, we have no correct name for it.

Paul Soldner

It may indeed be that we have no correct name for the "raku" made in the West, yet many people use the word and feel that it identifies a certain range of work which has certain consistent characteristics. As Hobart Cowles, Professor of Ceramics at the School for American Craftsmen, Rochester, writes: "Raku is raku—it probably comes closest to earthenware, but none that I am aware of could be called stoneware . . ." It is probable that the word "raku" is a genuinely useful collective title, like a national adjective such as "Japanese." Such words describe a generally accepted group of qualities, which obtain general consent and use, though it may be difficult to itemize their component parts.

Thinking of raku in general brings a few obvious characteristics immediately to mind. Soldner's original intention in 1960 was not to revive for the sake of reviving, but to pursue a new direction. His interest in pots that are relatively small, soft, and fragile has led to many technical and aesthetic directions in raku, and for many potters this smallness of scale has remained a dominant characteristic. Softness, gentleness, and avoidance of unpleasantly assertive tendencies remain a noticeable quality in much contemporary raku.

One technical factor comes immediately to mind too. During the post-firing process, time generally influences the potter and the pots. While this is true of other media, such as hot glass work, to some extent, raku remains exceptional in the range of alterations which can be made to a piece within a very short time. This factor is a decisive one in raku and requires some special mental preparation for the acts which have to be performed so quickly, as discussed in Chapter 6 on post-firing.

Verbalizing about raku seems to lead to paradoxes, as its very nature is paradoxical. For example, the results of the raku process may look rough but are refined; the potter makes use of random events, but plans; simplicity is so difficult to achieve—the pot may look crudely constructed, but it must be well crafted, otherwise it cracks; the procedure involves relaxation and concentration—the process is speedy, but represents much thought; it is not highly technical, yet it requires great experience and know-how. Perhaps this paradoxical element may explain why many potters like to glaze their pots partially with a white glaze: when smoked, these pots may become a resolution of the opposites, black and white. Probably the greatest paradox, though, is the incorporation of planned accident in the pieces.

To search for a further definition may seem trivial to some. Many potters doing impressive work in raku do not care about defining and analyzing the process; they work well without philosophical inquiries. But for those who may feel that it is the virtue of knowledge to impart control over experience, an investigation of the nature of the process they are working in can give firmness and confidence to convention and experiment alike.

Raku is often recognizable; it is technical in its way; it depends on accident, certainly. But can one say that there is some idea or process which includes all the pots now termed "raku," from Chojiro to Soldner, from Kenzan to Higby? Does raku have a specific nature to which all the activities dealt with in this book have an ultimate reference?

Some Approaches to a Definition

Often serviceable is a technical or historical method of definition which has the advantage of being verifiable and precise. Rhodes' excellent definition in the first edi-

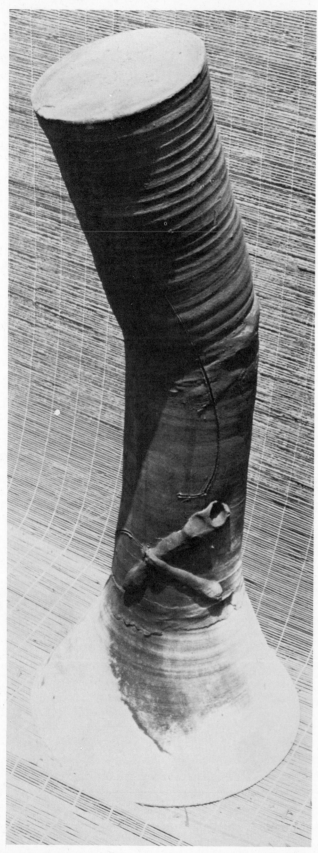

Raku Form by Howard Yana-Shapiro. 40" (101.6 cm) high. Thrown and altered, unglazed, smoked.

tion (1957) of *Clay and Glazes for the Potter* is typical of this approach. He defines raku as a "procedure for making pottery rather than a special color or glaze effect. . . . The technique was developed and used by the Japanese potters for making tea ceremony wares." Since 1957, both the procedures and the history have changed so much that to talk of a single procedure, which embraces that used by the original Raku family and everybody since Soldner, is almost impossible. As the procedures in what is termed raku are altering literally every day, a technical definition might be limited solely to an inclusion of a reference to the relatively low temperature of the firing, and the rapid heating and cooling. To say only this about raku, though, seems to leave unsaid all of the expressive qualities of the medium.

Paul Soldner, and many potters have agreed with this, has said that raku is not a technique at all, but an attitude. This represents an evolution of his understanding of raku, for he says that as late as 1967–68 he may have still felt that raku *was* a technique. Soldner thinks that his workshops up to that time may have disseminated that idea, but he is "now trying to live it down!" His present thinking on this point explains the nature of the addi-tude: "Raku for me is more a state of mind, a way of thinking, perhaps even a way of life, than a technique or a process." Soldner feels that his raku philosophy makes him open rather than closed, allows him to accept rather than demand, and that he now is able to achieve a going with, and bending, rather than the domineering control that he once sought. To illustrate his point, he referred to the belief held by Joan Campbell, the Austrailian potter, that raku has gentleness in the sense of softness and fra-gility, but not weakness. Raku, she feels, is like a person in this: some people are hard, brittle, and cannot stand shock in their lives, whereas raku is like a person who can stand much shock, having resilience and gentleness. Campbell admits to finding the inspiration for her work in the limestone oceanside landscape and intense light of Western Australia, and in the softness of sand underfoot. The ideas of the abrasive softness of beach sand, and of softness yet resilience to shock, perfectly express the union of fact and philosophy which many potters find in raku.

The majority of raku potters seem to favor this atti-tudinal definition, as summed up in Ken Vavrek's con-cise statment: "Raku has a visual quality suggesting a mystical or universal force certainly related to the proc-ess."

There are dissenters, however. Some potters are care-ful to de-romanticize raku, so to speak, apparently wish-ing to correct indulgent misunderstandings before they arise. Wayne Higby says, "I see raku as *just* another way of making pottery. *No* better than any other process. For me there is really no great value in the process except as it gives the artist a means of achieving an image." Joan Campbell writes of the unromantic finish to a day's fir-ing, when the potter is "covered in smoke and oil dirt,

Raku Bowl (above) *by John Chalke.*
Salmon glaze, thrown and altered.

Plate by Marguerite Antell.
Slab construction, white glaze
with crackle.

Vase by Paul Soldner. Thrown and altered, slab added, unglazed, engobes and metal oxides, smoked.

hair singed, nails broken, body dehydrated." Art Haney is less romantic yet: "I wouldn't classify my work as raku. I would call my work 'hot ware.'"

While not being a conclusive definition, the attitudinal approach to raku currently held by the majority of raku potters has evolved as a better way of looking at the subject than any technical or historical definition. Though, in a strict sense, there may be no true definition for the body of work usually termed "raku," the work created in the evolving process known by the term probably has its essential nature in an attitude. This attitude has close connections with the ability to accept and utilize the unexpected events that the earth can offer. This cooperation with the accidental can bear some further investigation in its turn, as discussed below.

Accident

While accident has been stressed earlier insofar as it is related to actions, we want to deal with it briefly here in more abstract and general terms.

Whenever the raku potter has occasion to choose to exercise control over his materials and his process, he is close to one of the essential situations in raku and, some would say, in life. To choose to control an event is momentous, irrespective of the importance of the particular event. To allow an accident to happen is equally momentous, and is, equally, a choice; it is part of the nature of raku to make such choices. By far the majority of raku pieces take their character essentially from the occurrence of surface accidents which happen during the glaze firing or post-firing. The acceptance of, or cooperation with, these accidents becomes an art. Indirectly, the acts of post-firing become transferred to other elements in the pot, such as to the form. The experienced potter, in forming a raku piece, is aware roughly of what might happen to the pot, and responds to this foreknowledge expressively with an appropriate form. The accidents of the post-firing, then, can determine the pot as a whole.

The physical details of accidents have been dealt with in Chapter 6 on post-firing. Certainly a familiarity with the likely outcome of a firing is an advantage, but accidents are by definition unexpected, and understanding and accepting the *idea* of an accident is perhaps the greatest difficulty. In ordinary language, an accident is something that would have been avoided if it could have been foreseen. It is probably unfortunate both in its results and also in the *fact* that it was not foreseen. (There can be "lucky" accidents, but the phrase is often used as an oxymoron, as though accidents occasionally produce exceptions to their own rules.) We like to be able to predict, to anticipate, and even pleasant surprises may be a blow to our self-esteem—perhaps this is why it sometimes takes an effort to realize that an unexpected result can be better than what we planned. In raku, unforeseen events will happen, but the process has not been evolved so that they may be cancelled easily. The raku pot may be re-

deemed from accident not by counteraction but by acceptance of its inevitability. Once having recognized the fact that events out of his control may complete his raku pots, the potter will face many questions. How is an accident good? Should he attempt to duplicate a lucky accident? Can any accident be good? Such questions may be puzzling but are also alluring.

The first pure accident will probably occur too fast for the potter to participate in it at all. Sometimes this is a good thing and sometimes not. However, after one has worked with raku for a while, as with anything, one develops "hunches" as Paul Soldner calls them, "kan" as the Japanese call it—intuition. Below the level of conscious thought, one has a feeling that a certain thing may happen and one makes instinctive preparations. This is probably one explanation for the interaction between the potter and the raku process. Heeding these intuitions is not easy and may come only with experience.

Even in accepting the idea of hunches, however, there is a chance that the potter may reject those events he did not have a hunch about. Pure accidents may remain chaotic intrusions in our familiar world. In recorded history, however, there have been a number of accepted beliefs that do not consider any event to be chaotic or accidental, and it is interesting to apply one of these to the question of accidents in raku.

The Chinese *Book of Changes* (in some editions with an introduction by C. J. Jung, see Bibliography) is older than Confucius. It is partly a soothsaying book, and it depends for its validity on totally random actions. In these actions, Jung sees what he calls an "acausal connecting principal": in other words, a connection between events not related by the cause and effect logic recognized by traditional Western thought. The book contains a number of oracular statements; each statement and its identifying sign of six lines is called a hexagram. The hexagram is "chosen" purely by random actions, such as throwing coins or selecting straws. The chance of the individual, perhaps his body's tensions, the moment itself, and the individual's predelictions in interpreting the message contained in his hexagram, are all felt to coincide meaningfully. The coincidence of random events with or through an individual's actions is felt to reveal a fundamental, universal pattern, and the incorporation of random events, far from invalidating the oracle, is essential to it. Using the *Book of Changes*, especially in an accurate edition, can give a queer feeling of hidden relationships which integrate random events. The point of mentioning it here in relation to raku is threefold. Firstly, it is Oriental and raku retains enough of its origins to puzzle the Occidental person. Secondly, the *Book of Changes*, with its commentary by Jung, is one of the more prestigious documents relating to the accidental. Thirdly, the attitude required for its use is in some respects similar to that required for raku and using it helps one understand the idea and place of accident, and our relationship to it.

The existence of such a philosophic attitude in history

Tailed Quincuplets by Carol Townsend. 13" (33) long, each. 1970. Thrown, pulled tails, luster glazes.

Three Goblets by Anne Mortimer. Thrown and altered, silver-white glaze.

may provide a model for the kind of philosophy being formed today with regard to some pottery. Many potters are no longer interested in completely predictable methods of making pots; they are less interested in perfect forms or effects; by implication they are less sympathetic with cause and effect logic than in the past, and more interested in using accidents in their work.

Here is where the existence of a fully evolved attitude in the Orient can be of assistance to the West. Both the sophisticated and unsophisticated wares of the best Oriental potters have already been influential in contributing their wise ignorance of cause and effect to their Western heirs. The Oriental potter apparently accepted chance effects as incidental to nature, not accidental to man.[1]

Besides demonstrating to the Western mind an alternative way of interpreting events, such works as *The Book of Changes* also provide a caution. The contemporary Western potter in raku who is already inclined to accept the incorporation of accident in his work may apply the idea with too much license, as he lacks the correctives available to his Oriental counterpart. For example, the view that cause and effect may be an illusion and exact prediction is undesirable, that carrying an idea through to the end, or even maintaining continuous personal supervision over events, is fruitless and too restricting. Many people like (or dislike) raku out of a misunderstanding of the nature of accident, and sometimes a novice may think that one accident is as good or bad as any other, and that metaphysical chaos excuses sloppy craftsmanship and lack of dedication. As Hobart Cowles puts it, "There is much of the accidental involved in raku and the novice may well produce an occasional 'great' piece and if he chooses to think so, all of his pieces may be 'great.' "

In cases such as these, *The Book of Changes* provides a model for the restrictions on this question of accident. Whatever one feels about the prophetic value of *The Book of Changes*, and many people are naturally sceptical, its use does invite, as Jung says, "one long admonition to careful scrutiny of one's own character, attitude, and motives." Insofar as the user of *The Book of Changes* has to interpret his own oracle, which is partly the result of his chance actions, as honestly as he can, the mental attitude required is analogous to that required for the judgment of chance effects on a "great" raku pot. Just as *The Book of Changes* did not reflect a valueless society, but one where, on the contrary, ethical behavior was highly valued, so raku may be developed as an attitude which involves severe judgments, discipline, and integrity. The self-scrutiny and honesty mentioned above by Jung is an essential part of the power of accepting chance in one's life and art. In raku, one has to use honestly the faculties of perception and develop the self-discipline of one's craft. Paul Soldner makes this point as follows:

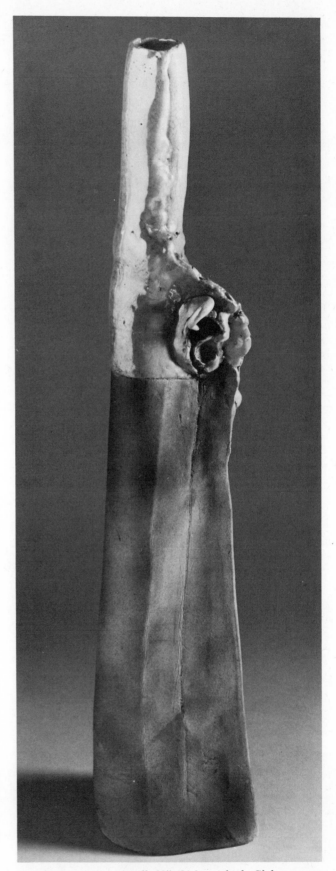

Vase by Marguerite Antell. 32" (81.3 cm) high. Slab construction, partially glazed and smoked.

One cannot accept accidents [sic] as an art itself, though I be-
lieve it's done. The accidents that happen in traditional historical
raku, don't happen to beginners. It happens to people who have
become so disciplined and so deeply involved, so on top of their
art, their craft, that then they are able to transcend the tech-
niques, they are able to be free to accept accidental or spontane-
ous results. . . . As (raku) grew out of the Zen religion we must
keep in mind that the freedom, the liveliness, the surprise, the
quality of freshness and vitality in Zen almost always grew out
of a very strong discipline.

It remains a fascinating challenge and a major paradox
in raku to realize that "accidental" effects can become
the essence of the piece, yet they cannot be guaranteed;
that they can come without the potter doing anything, yet
they are not easily achieved; that the best effects may be
truly unexpected, yet can have self-discipline and control
as their basis. Furthermore, such effects can be the starting point for the next pot without losing their vitality and
freshness. The "feel" for this process may be as difficult
to gauge, however, as the difference between advice and
interference.

While discussing the idea of accident, it is interesting
to note that the philosophies of many craftsmen seem to
fit a pattern. Wayne Higby may be most typical in this
respect when he says, "Responsive control is what I'm interested in, not absolute control. Therefore, the accidental accurancies[2] [sic] of the firing can be exciting, used,
looked forward to, and possibly even planned. . . ." On
the same topic, Paul Soldner is fond of using the word
"serendipitous" to express what he feels is the essence of
raku. Hobart Cowles also writes: "I think the accomplished raku craftsman exercises greater influence on the
accidental and that is about all any potter does." Most
raku potters seem to have chosen this medium because
they wish to explore or use the possibilities of accident
and the self-discipline it demands. None of them seems
to operate on a basis of raw luck. Higby again typifies this
firmness of attitude when he writes: "I do not expect my
work to rise or fall on the accidental happenings of a firing." The use of accident in raku, as understood by most
raku potters seems to be based on similar grounds to its
use in *The Book of Changes* in that accidents are felt to be
neither aberrations nor a sign of incompetence or lack of
control. On the contrary, the use of accident seems to recognize the limitations of humans to predict. In consort
with self-discipline and integrity, in raku the possibilities
of accident free the individual potter and his work, adding fresh vitality and spontaneity to his raku pots.

Spontaneity and Involvement

Closely tied to the incorporation of accident in a raku
piece is the idea of spontaneity. The opportunities for
spontaneity afforded by the processes of modern raku

have attracted many potters. Ken Vavrek moved from
low-fired whiteware, which he felt was slow, to raku because he "wanted more spontaneity." Daniel Rhodes
said that the speed of the process gives a psychological
advantage to the potter in raku, for he can glaze and fire
in one afternoon, seeing the results while the ideas he has
are still fresh; not only that, but the ideas can move from
pot to pot more quickly. Raku's informality attracts
many potters who work predominantly in other ceramic
media. Henry Gernhardt says, "I do not use the raku
method to make raku but to fulfill my need to explore a
broader philosophy, art. The raku method provides me
with a certain tempo of working, glaze and clay characteristics [sic] that no other method in ceramics provides."
The demands of spontaneity are fairly obvious. If the results of it are not to seem merely slapdash and hurried,
the concentrated relaxation and self-discipline spoken of
earlier need to be present.

The possibilities for self-expression are connected with
the principle of spontaneity. The direct experience that
raku offers, and the freeing and loosening spoken of
above, has attracted many potters. Many of those who
have written to us have expressed a deep involvement
with their pots in raku, and have compared the medium
favorably in this respect with less simple firing methods.
One potter, Nancy Baldwin, writes that before she did
raku: "I was like a mother who is totally out while giving
birth. With the discovery of raku, all this changed. I was
midwife to my own pot during its birthing."

No one, however, is more intense on this point of deep
involvement than Howard Yana-Shapiro:

The quality of black and white. The abstract quality. Monochro-
matic. The reduction and the glaze. Only white glaze. Even now
some pieces with no glaze. Only the fire.

As I sit and watch the fire, I become the flame. Itself. The fire.
Consumption. Concentration. My work. The heat. The reaction
of my body and mind. The moments of tension as the kiln is
raised. The pots taking the fire within. The heat off the pots.
Reaching in and lifting the pots out. The strain of the large
pieces. Carrying the piece to reduction. The next fire. The reduc-
tion. The surface of the piece altered and drawn on by me and by
the process Raku. Thinking to return to the early freedom of my
childhood.

Many potters share Shapiro's tendency toward mystic-
ism through raku, which is not always directed to nature
as one might expect, as much as it is directed toward the
inferno in the kiln.

That raku should have been revived when it was may
appear inevitable in a way: it is direct and experimental
where other processes in pottery are more remote and
theoretical; this directness leads to, almost requires, non-
conceptualization and spontaneity, and encourages "involvement"—the slogan word of a generation. In its
weaknesses and its strengths, raku might be the emblem
of that generation.

Deep Cove, Landscape Storage Jar by Wayne Higby. 13″ x 13″ x 10″ (33 x 33 x 25.4 cm). 1973. Earthenware, raku. This classical form with an individualized image is a superb example of the dialog between control and chance in raku.

Black Raku Incense Burner by Kit-Yin Tieng Snyder. 8" x 8" x 10" (20.3 x 20.3 x 25.4 cm). 1971. Slab construction.

Raku Plate by John Chalke. Slab construction, blue and white glazes, smoked. Chalke was trained in England and has frequently been to Japan and Korea. His work shows a strong personality absorbing many influences.

Tendencies toward Abstract Expressionism

When I am in my painting, I'm not aware of what I'm doing. It is only after a sort of get-acquainted period that I see what I have been about. I have no fears of making changes, destroying the image etc., because the painting has a life of its own. I try to let it come through. It is only when I lose contact with the painting that the result is a mess. Otherwise, there is pure harmony, an easy give and take, and the painting comes out well.

My painting does not come from the easel. . . . I prefer to tack the unstretched canvas to the wall or floor. I need the resistence of the hard surface. On the floor I am more at ease. I feel nearer, more a part of the painting, since in this way I can walk around it, work from the four sides, and literally be in the painting.[3]

The essence of these statements might well have been made by a contemporary potter about raku. The same elements are asserted—among them the bodily relationship between the artist and his work and the use of spontaneity of expression. Yet these comments were made by Jackson Pollock at the height of the Abstract Expressionist movement in the 1950s. Much work in raku can be typified according to criteria which apply to Abstract Expressionism—constant movement and shifting interrelationships in the elements of the work, particularly as time plays a part in the execution. There is a direct use of materials for their intrinsic value, for example, color and the tactile qualities of clay. Rather than an end product being the purpose of the work, sufficient purpose is provided by the record of the act of painting itself. The finished work is the record of acts in time, more than an image of something else. A painting becomes just that—a painting. Balance, form, color are all important, particularly in their psychological effect. Raku became popular when the influence of Abstract Expression was flowing to other media, and much raku still retains as part of its nature the immediate tendencies of its American revival.

The first of Pollock's statements above is also interesting in its stress on the complete absorption of the artist in his activities, on the unity between him and the painting, on the harmony and ease of the recording experience. Many elements in his statements could apply, not only to Abstract Expressionism, but also to art activities influenced by an Oriental religion, such as Zen Buddhism. Indeed, connections between Zen and Abstract Expressionism have been suggested. If indeed there is an intrinsic connection between the two aesthetics, then this explains their compatibility in raku. While certain contemporary potters in raku are concerned more than others to maintain some philosophical responsibility and connection with the original Japanese raku, many incorporate in their work the twin and often indivisible influences of Zen and of Abstract Expressionism.

Expansion of the Raku Process

We have noted previously that many potters experiment and take chances in order to preserve the balance be-

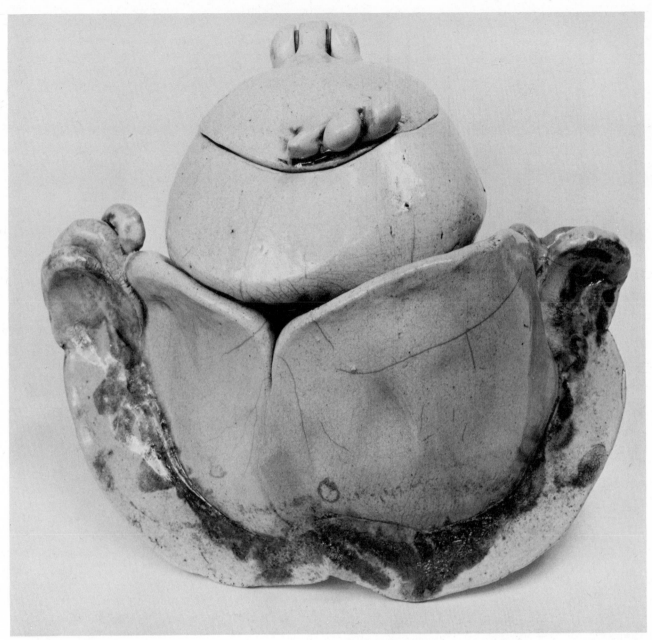

Box-on-a-shelf *by Nancy Jurs. 16" (40.6 cm) wide. 1974. Thrown and slabbed. Colemanite glazes, metal oxide decoration. Jurs' work is often whimsical in function and imagery.*

Vase *by Josh Nadal. 12″ (30.5 cm) high. Thrown, white and orange glaze, silver and copper luster.*

Lidded Box by Laureen Shaw. 1974. Thrown and slabbed, green-red copper glaze, reduced.

Raku Box by Richard Hirsch. 4″ x 4″ x 6″ (10.2 x 10.2 x 15.2 cm). 1971. Slab impressed, clear glaze fumed with iron and tin chloride. The functional aspect of this pot is secondary to the softness of its slab construction.

Covered Box by Adele Zimmerman. 5 3/4″ x 10″ (14.6 x 25.4 cm). Slab construction, colemanite glazes. There is a hard-edge element in both the form and the decoration.

tween spontaneity and control. As a result, the raku process has been expanded far beyond that invented by Chojiro, and even beyond that generally attributed to Soldner for his first raku pots in 1960. The continual evolution of procedure seems to be an attribute of the raku attitude.

Size has always been an important determining factor in the raku process. In his first pots Soldner reacted against the contemporary taste for big pots, and to some extent, raku is still believed to be suitable only for small ware. But as early as the mid-1960s, many potters, notably Steven Kemenyffy and David Middlebrook, increased the scale of their raku. With increased size came the need for many technical advances, principally caused by problems of removing the hot ware from the kiln. New kiln designs and materials were worked out, with ingenious car and barrel kilns becoming the most common. These used the basic idea that the kiln is moved away from the pot, not the pot from the kiln. Many potters, however, designed special tongs, as did the original raku potters, to enable them to carry awkward, medium-sized pots away from the kiln. To cope with pots of widely differing shapes, castable materials were used so that the kiln could be easily reconstructed to admit a drastically different pot (see Chapter 5 on kilns).

Increased size also led to the alteration of clay bodies to include high-lithia, non-clay materials, such as petalite or spodumene, which reduce thermal shock in the large pots (see Chapter 4 for more information on clay bodies). The post-firing process was modified, some potters digging holes in the ground for reduction containers, others using large barrels.

Gradually, the repertoire of raku glazes grew, until, from a total reliance on high lead-based glazes, raku potters moved into nontoxic substances such as alkaline frit, gertsley borate, and borax base glazes. The use of soluble salts (such as copper chloride, or cobalt chloride) both under and over the glaze increased the available color range. Underglazes, overglazes, and lusters, made from such seldom used materials as silver and bismuth nitrates, have been added. Raku has also lent itself to multiple firings (see Chapter 4 for more information on glazes).

Burner technology has been simplified until most potters can make their own out of basic plumbing supplies. A new material called Fiberfrax has been found to perform most successfully as a refractory substitute, and has greatly facilitated kiln building (see Chapter 5 for more information on kilns).

The number of combustible reducing agents has also expanded almost without limit. Though sawdust remains the old standby, the vastly increased range of combustibles is producing a larger variety of surface effects and has given greater control. Soldner did not use crackled glazes to any great extent, but they soon became a standard feature of raku. This effect has been relied on too of-

Raku Vase *by Joan Campbell. 18″ x 16″ (45.7 x 40.6 cm). Feldspar and mica surface. A unique surface quality achieved with the use of mica flecks on a rough, unglazed clay body.*

ten, but some potters, notably Higby and Shapiro, are still exploring crackle and its accidental pattern with force and originality.

There have been a few highly personal techniques still called raku, the most notable being Wayne Higby's inlaying of Egyptian paste in earthenware. Also, Paul Soldner recently began to place salt in his kiln, which fumes the clay, giving it gentle, warm tinges of color, without any of the orange-peel texture normally associated with a salt glaze.

All these technical advances and extensions of the basic process have become part of the nature of raku, especially so for those potters in whose work a close rapport with the material and a feeling for the process are strong elements. It has sometimes been suggested to us that raku is not very technical. Certainly, it is not generally as technical as multifired ware, for example, but technical discoveries have played a part in the history of the process, though to some people the directness of the experiences of raku may seem to overshadow this. Understanding clay chemistry is necessary to get the right clay body, which is open, has a low melting point, and fires to the desired color. Glaze chemistry in raku is just as complicated as in any other temperature range. Also, just as when Paul Soldner saw the pepper leaves and *knew* they would provide a reduction atmosphere to give his pots more subtlety, the potter can avoid losing the chance for many effects if he knows technical theories in advance. Above all, as Hobart Cowles has pointed out: "When [the raku craftsman] decides to 'reproduce' a great piece, then he becomes involved with influencing the accidental and then it becomes technically demanding." Raku can be as technical as the potter wants to make it.

To summarize the importance to the nature of raku of technical developments, it is possible to say that these developments have come about spontaneously, and usually with the purpose of exploring the possibilities for spontaneity in the process itself. It is likely that, the nature of the essential confrontation in raku being what it is, the raku process will continue to develop and expand until the degree of spontaneity involved ceases to provide craftsmen with the kind of stimulus they wish to work with.

Raku and Funk

One recent trend which has shown raku's limitations to some extent is the funk movement, now perhaps on the wane. While sharing with raku a reaction against symmetry and functionalism in ceramics, funk is heavily involved in the realm of conceptual art. In many cases, funk requires an exact physical replica of the potter's *idea* to be manifested in the pot. It may appear to be more spontaneous than it is. The conceptual element in funk is probably at variance with the mainstream development of raku as we see it, possibly because of the technical na-

ture of the process; most funk potters require a high degree of predictability from their medium. Bill Stewart exemplifies this: he began working in raku quite early but left it because he wanted more control.

Misconceptions

As we have said, while many potters admit to a philosophy of raku involving natural imagery or a sense of the natural, direct, humanness of the process, they are often hesitant about the connotations of such views. Higby is a good example, for though his imagery is unabashed landscape which is personally meaningful, he remains agnostic about a philosophical element which it would be all too easy to romanticize. His landscapes recall the hills and streams of Colorado, where he spent his childhood, yet, as we noted, he chooses raku only because it provides him with the imagery he needs. There may be a cautionary note here, for it is so easy to overdo the communion with nature, the rhapsodies over wood firing or other natural paraphernalia which might seem prerequisites for rakuing. It may indeed be that one reason for the kind of popularity that raku has had is that it does offer a release from technologically ordered thinking. Raku offers a rediscovery of elementary physical laws and their beauty and this may be attached to a reaction against urban environments. However, overemphasis on life-style change and reaction against an urban environment, can lead to one of the most pernicious misconceptions about raku: that to go into nature, wedge the clay with your feet, fire with wood and your friends, or go on a special diet, automatically guarantees strong, free raku pots. It may help some people to do these things, but they are not necessarily connected with raku, and good raku can be made anywhere.

Another misconception quite widely held about raku is that it is for beginners only. It is difficult to say how this started, though it may have been through Warren Gilbertson's 1942 article, "Making of Raku Ware and its Value in the Teaching of Beginner's Pottery in America" (see Chapter 1), and may persist because of the simple equipment and a misunderstanding of the reliance on accident. Beginners certainly can do raku and, moreover, do it quickly, the rapid process ensuring that the pots cool before their enthusiasm or ideas; in this respect, the use of raku as an introduction to ceramics in general is in many ways a good teaching device. Students do see the whole process in a short time, they do learn to feel what happens in a firing, and their efforts with each pot remain vivid in their memories. Raku is only deceptively easy, however, and sometimes the deception is not revealed in time, compounding the feeling that since the course began with raku, it is only for beginners. A remedy for this might be to tell the students, as Art Haney does, that when they have learned more and are ready, they can go back to raku.

Conclusions

The conclusion for a book of this kind usually involves a prediction for the future; this book is no exception, although predictions in any field seem particularly difficult at the time of writing. The direction of raku in the future is tied to the economic situation, the future of the craft movement, and the direction of ceramics in particular.

The increasingly technical nature of much ceramics in recent years might be viewed by some as an ironic development in view of the origins of the craft movement. The original reaction against manufactured ware produced in large quantities has been replaced to some extent by a heavy reliance (in, for example, high-fired reduction pieces and multi-fired luster ware), on technology, even for one-of-a-kind pieces. Yet raku may be one of a few experiments that continues the original instinctive reasons for crafted ware. Such experiments revive some of the more "primitive" processes and are responses to an urgent, contemporary, yet apparently timeless, need to impose the mark of the human hand on materials. Revivals such as wood firing are typical of this reponse, as potters discover the type of control a good familiar kiln can give over accidental ash-glaze effects. Daniel Rhodes has mentioned that there is a movement in California to begin Tamba-style firings. Salt glazing has become popular for similar reasons, and other more primitive methods are gaining attention. Paulus Berensohn has popularized pinching and sawdust firing—two of the most simple methods possible in ceramics, allowing maximum contact with the clay, and producing simple yet satisfying decorative effects from the firing. All these methods derive their strength from much the same source as raku—they rediscover a technical alternative which is also a philosophic alternative, based on the *use* of events, not on the domination over them. If we suppose that the revival of so-called "primitive" methods is going to be a main direction in ceramics, then it is fair to suppose that raku will be in the vanguard of such developments, being, as it is, one of the earliest of such processes to be extensively revived. If the revival of more "primitive" ceramic methods continues and dominates, raku may provide the model for the acceptance of accident and related adjustments of attitude.

Raku at present has established itself as a major art pottery medium, with certain potters devoting their time almost exclusively to it. Their work in its scale and reference is causing the older misconceptions about raku to die, and is establishing a classic vocabulary for the medium both in surface effects and in related forms. Raku now has its own tradition in the West, offering options which extend both a guideline and a challenge.

Simply to respond to the materials and the process would seem to be an easy thing to do, but to rise to the opportunity with calm self-discipline, freedom, ease, and contentment is the challenge to every potter who wants to work in raku.

River by Kit-Yin Tieng Snyder. 28" (71.1 cm) long. 1974. Slab construction, two parts, green and black glaze, smoked.

Notes

Chapter 1

1. There is a Zen saying that "One who knows does not speak, and the one who speaks does not know."

2. R. Tsunoda in *Sources of Japanese Tradition*. Ed. W.T. DeBary. Vol. 1, p. 234.

3. Y. Kojiro, *Forms in Japan*.

4. *Sources of Japanese Tradition*, p.279.

5. *Tea Taste in Japanese Art* (exhibition catalog), p.7.

6. *Sources of Japanese Tradition*, p. 233.

7. Sadler says he was the son of a Chinese. See *Cha-No-Yu: The Japanese Tea Ceremony*, p. 70.

8. Technical information was kindly supplied in a letter to the authors by Mutsuo Yanagihara, a contemporary Japanese potter. The letter was translated by Prof. H. Harootunian of the University of Chicago.

9. Black raku is glaze fired in the modern raku factory in Kyoto at cone 9 for 2½ minutes! It is placed in the hot kiln, timed with a stop watch, and withdrawn promptly. It is cooled quickly and as a result the body suffers from dunting, (cracking throughout the pot), which in the case of black raku gives it the distinctive dull sound when struck. Only an extremely strong clay body can withstand this treatment.

10. For a more complete account of these two potters, see Leach, *Kenzan and his Tradition* (London, 1966).

11. H.H. Sanders, *The World of Japanese Ceramics*, p. 192.

12. This opinion was also expressed in the letter referred to previously (Note 8).

13. This was also from a letter to the authors by Chalke.

14. From a letter to the authors by Bernard Leach.

15. Hester Jones, article in *El Palacio*, 1954.

16. The following account is a summary of part of a cassette recording made for the authors by Paul Soldner.

17. This information is contained in a letter to the editor of *Ceramics Monthly*, Sept. 1974, by Gillian Hodge. Accompanying the letter is a small photo of a tea bowl made by Riegger in 1957. The tea bowl appears to have a definite crackle which would be the result of the post-firing process now familiar to most raku potters. If so, and there is no reason to doubt Ms. Hodge's veracity, this would be one of the earliest examples of raku altered by a post-firing reduction atmosphere. There is still room for study to establish all the details of early raku in the United States.

Chapter 2

1. Johannes Itten from *Bauhaus Weimar 1919–25, Dessau 1925–28* (Boston: Branford, 1952), quoted in G. Naylor, *The Bauhaus* (London: Studio Vista, 1968), p. 62.

2. Gertrud and Otto Natzler, *Ceramics* (catalog of the Collection of Mrs. Leonard R. Sperry, Los Angeles County Museum of Art, 1968), p. 33.

Chapter 3

1. Gertrud and Otto Natzler, *Ceramics* (catalog of the Collection of Mrs. Leonard R. Sperry, Los Angeles County Museum of Art, 1968), p. 34.

Chapter 5

1. The procedure for building this kind of kiln was described in an article by Howard Shapiro and Randal Muchow in the Oct. 1973 issue of *Craft Horizons*.

Chapter 6

1. See Note 1, Chapter 5.

Chapter 7

1. B. Leach, *A Potter's Book*, p. 25.

2. We were interested in this word, coined for the occasion perhaps, in an eloquent and carefully prepared letter to us by the potter. The confusion of "occurences" and "accuracies" makes perfectly the point under discussion.

3. Eleanor C. Munroe, *Golden Encyclopedia of Art* (New York: Golden Press), p. 258.

Picture Credits

Suppliers List

Ceramic Colors and Frits

American Art Clay Co. (AMACO)
4717 W. 16th St.
Indianapolis, IND 46222

Ceramic Color and Chemical Mfg. Co.
P.O. Box 297
New Brighton, PA 15066

B.F. Drakenfield, Inc.
45 Park Pl.
New York, NY 10051 *or*
Washington, PA 15301

George Fetzer
1205 17 Ave.
Columbus, OH 43211

General Color and Chemical Co.
P.O. Box 7
Minerva, OH 44657

International Minerals and
Chemical Corporation
IMC Plaza
Libertyville, ILL 60048

Minnesota Clay Co.
2410 E. 38th St.
Minneapolis, MN 55420

Standard Ceramic Supply Co.
P.O. Box 4435
Pittsburgh, PA 15205

Trinity Ceramic Supply, Inc.
9016 Diplomacy Row
Dallas, TX 75247

Van Howe Ceramic Supply Co.
11975 E. 40 Ave.
Denver, CO 80239 *or*
4860 Pan American Freeway N.E.
Albuquerque, NM 87107

Western Ceramic Supply
1601 Howard St.
San Francisco, CA 94103

In Canada

Barrett Co. Ltd.
1155 Dorchester Blvd.
W. Montreal, Quebec, Canada (2)

Pottery Supply House
P.O. Box 192
Oakville, Ontario, Canada

Ceramic Equipment

A.D. Alpine Inc. (wheels, kilns, burners)
353 Coral Circle
El Segundo, CA 90245

Bluebird Mfg. Co. (pug mills)
c/o Judson Pottery
100 Gregory Rd.
Ft. Collins, CO 80521

Robert Brent Co.
(wheels, slab machines)
128 Mill St.
Headsburg, CA 95448

I.J. Cress Co., Inc. (kilns)
1718 Floradale Ave.
S.E. Monte, CA 91733

Crusader Industries, Inc. (kilns)
338 W. 12th St.
Holland, MICH 49423

Denver Fire Clay Co.
(wheels, kilns, burners)
P.O. Box 5507
Denver, CO 80217

Eclipse Fuel Engineering Corp.
1100 Buchanan St.
Rockford, ILL 61101

W.H. Fairchild (kilns)
712 Centre St.
Freeland, PA 18224

Flynn Burner Corp.
425 5th Ave.
New Rochelle, NY 10802

C.L. Gougler Machine Co. (pug mills)
805 Lake St.
Kent, OH 44240

Hauck Mfg. Co. (burners)
P.O. Box 26
Westchester, ILL 60153

HED Industries, Inc. (kilns)
Unique Kilns
Box 176
Pennington, NJ 08534

Johnson Gas Appliance Co. (burners)
Cedar Rapids, IA 52405

L and L Mfg. Co. (kilns)
Box 348
144 Conchester Rd.
Twin Oaks, PA 19104

The Max Corp. (wheels)
Box 34068
Washington, DC 20034

Maxon Premix Burner Co.
201 East 18th St.
Muncie, IND 47302

North American Burner
4455 E. 71st St.
Cleveland, OH 44125

Oscar-Paul Corp. (wheels)
522 W. 182 St.
Gardena, CA 92247

Paragon Industries, Inc. (kilns)
Box 10133
Dallas, TX 75207

Randall Wheel (wheels and clay mixers)
Box 774
Alfred, NY 14802

Shimpo (wheels)
Shimpo-West
P.O. Box 2315
La Puente, CA 91746

Skutt and Sons (kilns)
2618 S.E. Steele St.
Portland, OR 97202

Soldner Pottery Equipment
(wheels, clay mixers)
Box 90
Aspen, CO 81611

Walker Jamar Co. (pug mills)
365 South First Ave.
E. Duluth, MN 55802

Westwood Ceramic Supply Co.
(wheels, kilns, burners)
14400 Lomitas Ave.
City of Industry, CA 91744

In Canada

Estren Mfg. Ltd. (wheels, kilns, burners)
1767 W. 3rd Ave.
Vancouver, B.C. Canada

Refractories

Babcock and Wilcox Co.
161 E. 42nd St.
New York, NY 10017

Carborundum Co. (fiberfrax)
Box 337
Niagara Falls, NY 14302

Du Pont de Nemours & Co.
(shredded nylon)
1007 Market St.
Wilmington, DEL 19898

Eastern Refractories Co.
162½ Barrie St.
Montpelier, VT 05602

A.P. Green Co.
1018 E. Breckenridge St.
Mexico, MO 65265

Johns-Manville Co.
22 E. 40th St.
New York, NY 10016

La-Mo Refractory Supply Co., Inc.
323 Iris Ave.
P.O. Box 10325
New Orleans, LA 70121

Maryland Refractories Co.
Alexandria, PA 16611

New Castle Refractories Co.
P.O. Box 471
New Castle, PA 16103

North American Refractories Co.
1012 National City E. 6th Bldg.
Cleveland, OH 44114

General Ceramic Supplies

Bog Town Clay
75-J Mendel Ave. S.W.
Atlanta, GA 30336

Capital Ceramics, Inc.
2174 S. Main St.
Salt Lake City, UT 84115

Central Ceramics Art Supply Co.
29 W. 555 Batavia Rd.
Warrenville, IND 60553

Clay Art Center
40 Beech St.
Port Chester, NY 10573

Cole Ceramics Labs
Northeastern Ofc.
Box 248
Sharon, CONN 06069

Eagle Ceramics
12264 Wilkins Ave.
Rockville, MD 20852

Earthworks
420 Merchants Rd.
Rochester, NY 14609

Firehouse Ceramics
55 Prince St.
New York, NY 10012

Gare Ceramic Supply Co.
P.O. Box 830
165 Rosemont St.
Haverhill, MASS 01830

Greek-Farm Lab
Rt. 38
Hainesport, NJ 08036

Harriss Linden Ceramics
1772 Genessee Ave.
Columbus, OH 43211

House of Ceramics
1011 North Hollywood
Memphis, TN 38108

Langley Ceramic Studio
413 S. 24th St.
Philadelphia, PA 19146

L & R Specialties
120 S. Main
Box 373
Nixa, MO 65714

Leslie Ceramics Supply Co.
1212 San Pablo Ave.
Berkeley, CA 94706

Mandl Ceramic Supply Co.
R.R. #1
Box 369A
Pennington, NJ 08534

Miller Ceramics, Inc.
8934 N. Seneca St.
Weedsport, NY 13166

Newton Potters Supply
Box 96
West Newton, MASS 02165

Ohio Ceramic Supply, Inc.
Box 630
Kent, OH 44249

Pacifica Crafts
Box 1407 Dept. C
Ferndale, WA 98248

Paramount Ceramics, Inc.
220 N. State
Fairmont, MN 56031

Richland Ceramics
P.O. Box 4126
Columbus, SC 29204

Rovin Ceramics
6912 Shaefer
Dearborn, MICH 48126

Seeleys Ceramic Service, Inc.
9 River St.
Oneonta, NY 13820

Sculpture House
38 E. 30th St.
New York, NY 10016

Van Howe Ceramics Supply Co.
11975 E. 40th
Denver, CO 80239

Way-Craft
394 Delaware St.
Imperial Beach, CA 92032

Webco Supply Co.
Box 3504
Tyler, TX 75701

Jack D. Wolfe
724 Meecker Ave.
Brooklyn, NY 11222

In Canada

Clay Crafts Supply
1004 Taylor St.
Saskatoon, Sas., Canada

HIRO Distributors
518 Beatty St.
Vancouver, B.C., Canada

Clays—Bulk

A.P. Green Fire Brick Co.
1018 E. Breckenridge St.
Mexico, MISS 65265

Castle Clay Products
1055 S. Fox St.
Denver, CO 80223

Cedar Heights Clay Co.
50 Portsmouth Rd.
Oak Hill, OH 45656

Edgar Plastic Kaolin Co.
Edgar, Putnam Co., FLA 32049

Garden City Clay Co.
Redwood, CA 94064

Georgia Kaolin Co.
433 N. Broad St.
Elizabeth, NJ 07207

Kentucky-Tennessee Clay Co.
Box 447
Mayfield, KY 42066

Pacific Clay Products
Norwalk Ave.
Santa Fe Springs, CA 90670

Paoli Clay Co.
Rt. 1
Belleville, WS 53508

Spunks Clay Co.
Box 829
Paris, TN 38242

United Clay Mines Corp.
Trenton, NJ 08606

British Suppliers

E.J. Arnold & Sons Ltd.
Butterley St., Leeds 10

Craftsmen Potters Association
William Blake House, Marshall St.
London W.1

Ferro (Gt. Britain) Ltd.
Wombourne
Wolverhampton, Staffs

Fraser Ltd., Keramos
Parkside, Trentham
Stoke-on-Trent, Staffs

Fulham Pottery Ltd.
210 New Kings Rd.
Fulham, London S.W. 6

Harrison/Mayer Ltd. Meir
Stoke-on-Trent, Staffs

Larbert Supplies & Maintanence Ltd.
18 Main St.
Stirlingshire, Scotland

Podmore & Sons Ltd.
Shelton
Stoke-on-Trent, Staffs

Potclays Ltd.
Wharf St.
Stoke-on-Trent, Staffs

Pottery Centre of Ireland Ltd.
95 St Stephen's Green
Dublin 2, Ireland

South Wales Art & Craft Supplies
108 Bute St.
Cardiff

Bibliography

Berensohn, P. *Finding One's Way with Clay*. New York: Simon & Schuster, 1972.

Blaser, W. *Japanese Temples and Tea Houses*. New York: F.W. Dodge, 1956.

Cardew, M. *Pioneer Pottery*. London: Longmans, 1969.

Clark, R.J., M. Eidelberg, D.A. Hanks, S.O. Thompson, and others. *The Arts and Crafts Movement in America 1876–1916*. Ed. R, Judson Clark. Princeton University Press, 1972.

Davis, J.C. "Crackling Raku Glazes with Oil Reduction," *Ceramics Monthly*, Jan. 1974.

DeBary, W.T., ed. *Sources of Japanese Tradition*. New York: Columbia University Press, 1964.

Dickerson, J. *Raku Handbook: A Practical Approach to Ceramic Art*. New York: Van Nostrand Reinhold, 1972.

Engel, H. *The Japanese House–A Tradition for Contemporary Architecture*. Rutland: Chas. E. Tuttle, 1964.

Fairbank, J.K., E.O. Reischauer, A.M. Craig. *East Asia: Tradition and Transformation*. Boston: Houghton Mifflin, 1973.

Gilbertson, W. (See bibliography below.)

Grousset, R. *Chinese Art and Culture*. Trans. by H. Chevaher. New York: Grove Press, 1959.

Hodin, J.P. *Bernard Leach–A Potter's Work*. Evelyn Adams and McKay, distributed by Kodansha Int. of U.S.A., Palo Alto, 1967.

I Ching or Book of Changes. Trans. by R. Wilhem. Intro. C.J. Jung. Princeton University Press, 1950.

In Praise of Hands, Benson and Hedges (Canada) Ltd., Ontario Science Center, Toronto; McClelland and Stewart Ltd., W.C.C., 1974.

Jenyns, S. *Japanese Pottery*. London: Faber, 1971.

Jung, C.J. "Synchronicity: An Acausal Connecting Principle," *The Collected Works of C.J. Jung*, vol. 8. Trans. by R.F.C. Hull. Princeton University Press, 1960.

Kim, Dr. C., and G. St. G.M. Gompertz, eds. *The Ceramic Art of Korea*. New York: Thomas Yoseloff, 1961.

Kojiro, Y. *Forms in Japan*. Trans. by K. Yasuda. Honolulu: East-West Centre Press, 1965.

Leach, B. *A Potter's Book*. London: Faber, 1940; Levittown, NY: Transatlantic.

——— *A Potter in Japan*. London: Faber, 1960.

——— *Kenzan and his Tradition*. London: Faber, 1966.

Lee, S.H. *A History of Far Eastern Art*. New York and New Jersey. Abrams and Prentice-Hall, 1974.

Littleton, H.F. *Glassblowing: A Search for Form*, New York: Van Nostrand Reinhold, 1971.

Minamoto, H. *An Illustrated History of Japanese Art*. Trans. H.G. Henderson, Kyoto; Hoshimo, 1935.

Miura, Isshu and Ruth Fuller Sasaki. *The Zen Koan*. New York: Harcourt Brace, 1964.

Mitsuoka, Tadanari. *Ceramic Art of Japan*. Japan Travel Bureau, Tokyo.

Munro, E.C. *Golden Encyclopedia of Art*. New York: Golden Press, 1964.

Munsterberg, H. *The Ceramic Art of Japan*. Rutland: Chas. E. Tuttle, 1964.

Natzler, G. and O. *Ceramics*. Catalog of the Collection of Mrs. Leonard M. Sperry, Los Angeles County Museum of Art, 1968.

Naylor, G. *The Bauhaus*. London: Studio Vista, 1968.

Nelson, G. *Ceramics: A Potter's Handbook*. New York: Holt, Rinehart and Winston, 1971.

Nordness, L. *Objects: U.S.A.* New York: Viking Press, 1970.

Okakura, K. *The Book of Tea*. 1906. Reprint, Rutland: Chas. E. Tuttle, 1956.

Piepenberg, R. *Raku Pottery*. New York: MacMillan, 1972.

Reps, P. *Zen Flesh, Zen Bones*. New York: Doubleday, 1961.

Riegger, H. *Raku: Art and Technique*. New York: Van Nostrand Reinhold, 1970.

Rhodes, D. *Clay and Glazes for the Potter*. Philadelphia: Chilton, 1957. Rev. ed., 1973. London: Pitman, 1967.

——— *Kilns: Design, Construction and Operation*. Philadelphia: Chilton, 1968. London: Pitman, 1969.

Rosenberg, H. *The Tradition of the New*. New York: McGraw-Hill, 1965.

Sadler, A.L. *Cha-No-Yu: The Japanese Tea Ceremony*. Rutland: Chas. E. Tuttle, 1962.

Sanders, H.H. *The World of Japanese Ceramics*. Tokyo: Kodansha Int., 1967.

Sohitsu. *The Art of Taking Tea*. Kyōto: Tanko Shiusha Co.

Tea Taste in Japanese Art, New York: Asia House.

Wildenhain, M. *Pottery: Form and Expression*. New York: A.C.C. and Van Nostrand Reinhold, 1962.

——— *The Invisible Core: A Potter's Life and Thoughts*. Palo Alto: Pacific Books, 1973.

Yanagi, S. *The Unknown Craftsman*. Palo Alto: Kodansha Int., 1972.

Warren Gilbertson

Exhibits at the Art Institute of Chicago

1933	Jan 12–Mar 5	No. 7, p. 14
1935	Jan 31–Mar 10	No. 4, p. 15
	Oct 24–Dec 8	No. 1, p. 11
1936	Jan 20–Mar 1	No. 3, p. 14
1938	July 28–Oct 9	Vol. 1, no. 7, p. 4
	Oct 20–Dec 4	No. 2, p. 14
1940	Mar 14–Apr 14	No. 3, p. 13
1941	Nov 15–Dec 29	Gallery G15
1941	Catalog	708.1.C53

Written Material by Gilbertson

"Photographs and Notes on Traditional Japanese Handcraft Productions," 1942. Unpublished. One copy in Ryerson Library, Art Institute of Chicago. Stacks. D15.08.G46.

"Making of Raku Ware and Its Value in the Teaching of Beginners' Pottery in America" in *Bulletin of the American Ceramic Society*, vol. 22, no. 2, pp. 41–44.

Articles on Gilbertson

New Releases and This Week, Art Institute of Chicago, 1941. 708.1.C53n 77:112541. Review of his one-man show.

El Palacio, Santa Fe, N. Mexico: The School of American Research, The Museum of New Mexico, and the Laboratory of Anthropology. Jan. 1953, vol. 60, no. 1, p. 328; vol. 60, no. 9, p.328; and Apr. 1954, vol. 61, no. 4, pp. 118–119. Obit.

Glossary and Index

Numbers in italic refer to illustrations

Freer Collection, 27

Frisenda, John, kiln design by, *132*

Fritted glazes: alkaline, 84–89; lead, 81–83

Fuji-san, 20. Tea bowl made by Kōetsu.

Fuming, *73, 88.* Depositing a very thin layer of metal, such as ferric, silver, tin, or zinc chloride, on a glaze. In raku fuming is accomplished by one of two methods: (1) Introducing the chloride in liquid form into the kiln at the burner ports and blocking up all air intakes. In two or three minutes, the kiln can be opened and the pots removed. (2) Pulling the red-hot pots from the glaze firing and spraying a solution of metal chloride onto them.

Funk, 50, 165. An art movement that centers on social commentary, humor, and technical virtuosity in individual media.

"G" factor, 125. An indicator of the grade of softbrick.

Gas burners. *See* burners, gas

Gernhardt, Henry, *50, 128, 140, 141,* 156, *165*

Gerstley borate, 84, *103,* 162

Gilbertson, Warren (1910–1954), *19,* 22, 165

Glaze(s), 56, 71, 72, 77, 78, 80, 81, 83, 139; alkaline, 78, 83, 84–89; "boiling," 140; commercial, 92, 94–95, 145; fritted, 81–83, 84–89; iridescent, *31,* 89, 92; lead, 78–83; melt, 140; recipes, 77, 78, 81, 83, 85, 87, 89; traditional raku, 17. *See also* Crackle *and* Luster

Glaze firing. *See* Firing, glaze

Gold chloride, *108*

Golden Beetle, 18. Tea bowl attributed to Nonko.

Granite, 72

Greenware, 43. Unfired pottery.

Griffith, Jean, 26–27

Grog, 73, 77, 126

Hamada, Shōji, 25

Haney, Art, 145, *153,* 165

Hare's fur glaze, *12. See also* Tenmoku

Hay, used in post-firing, 143

Haystack School of Crafts, 27

Hearn, Lafcadio, 21

Hideyoshi, 17. Japanese military man who sponsored the tea ceremony (1536–1598).

Higby, Wayne, *34, 51, 55,* 149, 151, 156, *157,* 165

Hirsch, Richard, *31, 32, 46, 59, 70, 79, 82, 87, 108, 110–112, 144,* 162

Hygroscopic, 84. Capable of absorbing water from the surrounding air.

Ichinyu. *See* Raku family

Ieyasu, Tokugawa, 17. Japanese military man.

Iga, 17. A type of Japanese pottery.

Ikebana, 20. Japanese word for flower arranging.

"In Praise of Hands," World Craft Council Shows in Toronto, 47

Insulation, kiln. *See* kiln(s), raku: insulation

Iridescence, in glaze, *31,* 89, 92

Iron: chloride, *101, 110, 162;* in glaze, 17, 25, 78, 80, *97, 98,* 104

Jokei. *See* Raku family

Jordan clay, 77

Juko, Murata, 14. Japanese "father of the tea ceremony, (1423–1502 A.D.).

Jurs, Nancy, *42, 49, 86, 103,* 125, *141, 159*

Kamakura period, 15

Kamogawa stone, 17. Special stone from the Japanese river Kamo used to make a black glaze.

Kan, 153. Japanese word for intuition.

Kaneko, Jun, *99, 148*

Kaolin, 73, 96

Kaowool, *128.* A type of insulating material used for kilns.

Karatsu, 17. A type of Japanese pottery.

Kawai, Kanjiro, 22, 30

Kemenyffy, Steven, *30, 40, 52, 73, 88*

Kemenyffy, Susan, *30, 40, 52, 73, 88*

Kenzan, Ogata Kenzan I, 1663–1743 A.D., 20, 78, 99, 149. Japanese potter, great nephew of Kōetsu.

Kenzan, Ogāta Kenzan VI, 1853–1923, 20, 21

Kenzan VII. *See* Bernard Leach

"K" factor, 125. An indicator of the grade of softbrick.

Kiln(s), raku: catenary arch, *118,* 125; circular, *114;* corbeled arch, *122–123;* design, 115, 116, 119; electric, 119, 124; Fiberfrax Lo-Con felt insulated, *126, 127, 132;* firing time, *126, 127;* Kaowool, insulated, *128;* gas fired, 27, 116, *128, 130, 131;* insulation, 126, *127–128,* 132; loading, 138; metal drum, 126, *127;* oil fired, 119, *128,* 129; requirements, construction, and use, 113–128; shelves, 115, 116, *120,* 126–128; siting, 115, 116; solar energy, *135;* Vermiculite insulated, 77, 126; with welded frame, *114, 117. See also* Brick(s) *and* Burners

Kizaemon Ido, 17. Revered Japanese tea bowl.

Kōetsu, Honami, 20, 79. Japanese raku potter (1558–1637 A.D.).

Kōetsu, Koho, 20. Grandson of Honami Kōetsu.

Kurashiki Folk Craft Museum, 22

Lawson, Dave, 89

Leach, Bernard (Kenzan VII), 21–22, 29, 69, 78

Lead, 78, 80; carbonate, 80; monoxide, 80; silicate and monosilicate, 81; toxicity, 78, 80

Lead-based glazes, 78–83. *See also* Fritted glazes

Levine, Marilyn, *39*

Lithia, 77, 162

Luster, 49, *50, 73, 88,* 89, *90, 91,* 92, 144, *154, 160,* 162. Thin metallic coating on a glaze producing iridescence. *See also* Iridescence.

"Making of Raku Ware and Its Value in the Teaching of Beginners Pottery in America," 25, 165

Mica, in clay body, *80, 163*

Middlebrook, David, 162

Morris, William, 49

Mortimer, Ann. *117, 154*

Mortimer, Norman, *117, 154*

Muromachi period, 17

Nadal, Josh, *160*

Natzler, Otto, 38, 45, 56

Ninsei, 20. Japanese potter who developed overglaze enameled stoneware.

Nobunaga, Oda, 17. A Japanese military man.

Nonko. *See* Raku family

Oil burners. *See* Burners, oil

Oil drum, used for kiln, 126, *127*

Oilspot glaze, *See* Tenmoku

Oribe ware, *16,* 17

Overglaze, 162

Oxidation, 78

Oxide decoration, *58,* 80, *86,* 92, *152, 159*

Paley, Albert, *37*

Pbw. Parts by weight.

Pearlite, 77

Petalite, 77. A fluxing mineral that can be used as a source of lithia in glazes; related to spodumene.

Photographic decal, *41, 90, 91*

"Photographs and Notes on Traditional Japanese Handcraft Production." 22

Pinching, *58, 59,* 165

Pinch pot, 56, *59, 112*

Pioneer Pottery, 49

Plasticity, *61,* 73, 77. The property of moist clay that permits the shape to be deformed without cracking and to retain its new shape when the pressure is removed.

Plumbing supplies, *130–133*

Pollock, Jackson, 158

Post-firing, 21, 27, 71, 72, 76, 92, 137–147, 149, 165. *See also* Smoking

Potters Book, A, 21, 22, 25, 29–30; glaze recipes from, 78, 81

Pottery Northwest, 27

Propane burners. *See* Burners, gas

Propane gas, 116

QF-180, 126. Special glue for use with Fiberfrax Lo-Con Felt.

Raku, history, 11–27, 144. Japanese word signifying "pleasure," "enjoyment," "ease."

Raku family: Chojiro (first Raku), 17–18, 20, 149, 162; Ichinyu (fourth Raku), 20; influences, 18; Jokei (seventh Raku), 17, 18; Nonko (Donyu, third Raku), *10*, 18–20; Raku-san, 18, 20; Riyku, Sen-no, 15, 17–18, 20

Raku-san. *See* Raku family

Raku ware, traditional, 10, *13–15*

Rakuyaki, 20. Japanese word for raku ware.

Red raku, 18, 20

Reduction, 27, 48, 78, 89, 92, *109*, 115, *142, 144, 161. See also* Post-firing *and* Smoking

Refractory, 77, 125. Difficult to melt even at high temperatures.

Rhodes, Daniel, 25, 149, 156, 166

Riegger, Hal, 27, 114

Riyku. *See* Raku family

Safety in firing, 124, 138, 143

Sagger, 115

Salt: in glaze process, 105, 166, 167; vapor firing, *98, 106*

Samurai, 15. Japanese warriors.

Sand, used in clay body, 77

Sawdust, used in post-firing, 143, 162, 166

School for American Craftsmen, 49, 149

Sculptural pottery, 49–50, 54

Seattle Art Museum, 18

Sepo (White Cap), 20. Tea bowl made by Kōetsu.

Shaw, Laureen, *161*

Shino, 17. A type of Japanese pottery.

Short, 58. An open, heavily grogged clay body that lacks plasticity.

Shredded nylon, 77

Shrinkage, 72

Sijan, Marc, *41, 90, 91*

Silica, 73, 85

Silicic acid, 17

Silver nitrate, *100, 103*

Slab construction, *46, 58, 62, 63, 68,* 69, *70, 79, 87, 100, 101, 103, 108, 144, 151, 155, 158, 161, 162, 165, 168*

Slip(s), 17, 43, 96. Any clay mixed with water to a smooth consistency; now mainly used for decoration. *See also* Engobe

Smoking, *53, 54, 68,* 70, *87,* 89, *97,* 110, *112, 144, 150, 155, 158, 165, 168*. Part of the post-firing in raku when the red hot ware is pulled from the kiln and put in combustible material which ig-

nites and smolders. *See also* Post-firing *and* Reduction

Snyder, Kit-Yin Tieng, *49, 84, 158, 166*

Solar energy kiln, *135*

Soldner, Paul, *21, 22, 23–25,* 56, *58,* 80, *84, 93, 97, 98, 105–107,* 136, *140,* 143, 149, 150, *152,* 155, 156, 158, 162, 165, oil burner design, *129;* workshop, *146–147*

Soluble salts, 162. Salts, particularly sulphates of calcium, magnesium, and sodium present in some clays; when the clay is drier, these salts migrate to the surface. *See also* Cobalt chloride *and* Copper chloride

Spalling, 124. When flakes of material fall off a brick, thus weakening and eventually destroying it.

Spodumene. 77. A lithium mineral, similar to petalite.

Stewart, Bill, *34,* 165

Stoneware, *12,* 13, 20, 22, 27, *28,* 38, 47, 69, 72, 77, 78, *See also* Clay

Straw, used in post-firing, 143, *144*

Talc, 77

Target brick, 122. Brick placed in front of the burner in a kiln to deflect the flame from hitting the ware directly.

Tea bowls, 10–15, 18; Chien-yao ware, 17; Edo period, *10, 14, 15;* summer, *66–67;* Sung dynasty, *12;* winter, *64–65;* Yi dynasty, 17

Tea caddy, Oribe ware, *16,* 17

Tea ceremony, 11, 14, 15, *16,* 17

Teaism, 14–15. A Japanese cult of tea drinking and its attendant ceremony.

Tell, Dave, 77, 83, *136, 140*

Tenmoku, 14–17. Japanese name for a very dark colored, reduced iron stoneware glaze of the Chien Sung types, including hare's fur, oilspot, etc.

Texture, 32, 43

Thermal shock failure, 72, 77, 162

Throwing, 58, *62,* 69, *97, 98, 103,* 144, *145, 151, 154, 160*

Thrown and altered forms, *21, 46,* 58, *74, 79, 98, 111,* 144, *150–152, 154, 159, 161*

Tigertorch or weed burner, 129, *132, 134*

Tokyo Folk Craft Museum, 22

Tomimoto, Kenkichi, 21, 78. Japanese potter.

Tongs, 15, 124, *141,* 162

Tooth, 77. Coarse texture in clay body.

Toshiro, 17. Japanese potter.

Townsend, Carol, 87, 89, *154*

Toxicity in glaze, 78, 80

Underglaze, 73, 162

Unknown Craftsman, The, 45, 47

Vandengerge, Peter, 57

Vavrek, Ken, *57, 74, 75,* 77, *85,* 87, 150, 156

Venturi principle in gas burner, 132. An inspirating burner with a constricted flow just beyond the point where gas exits, thus increasing the speed of gas flow and drawing air in from behind it.

Vermiculite, 77, 126. An expanded mica which is fairly refractory; used as a heat insulator for raku temperature.

Wabi, 14–15, 18. Japanese word for "simple," "retiring," "austere"; school of tea, 17

Weed burner. *See* Tiger Torch

Wildenhain, Frans, *28,* 38, *48*

Wollastonite, 77. Calcium metasilicate in both natural and synthetic forms; can be used as a source of calcium in glazes.

Woodman, Betty, *50, 61, 81,* 118, *125,* 145

World Crafts Council, "In Praise of Hands," 47

Yanagi, Sōetsu, 17, 25, 45, 47

Yanaghihara, Mutsuo, 20, 21

Yana-Shapiro, Howard, *16,* 18, *30, 64–67, 144, 150,* 156

Yi period, 17

Yoshimitsu, Shogun Ashikaga, 11, Japanese ruler (1358–1408).

Yugen, 14. Japanese word for the ultimate quality in art.

Zen Buddhism, 11, 17, 29, 53, 156, 158

Zeze ware, *15*

Zimmerman, Adele, 77, 85, 87, 89, *162*

Edited by Sarah Bodine
Designed by Bob Fille
Set in 10 pt. Times Roman by Publishers Graphics, Inc.